The Merrill Studies
in
Invisible Man

Compiled by
Ronald Gottesman
Livingston College, Rutgers University

Charles E. Merrill Publishing Company
A Bell & Howell Company
Columbus, Ohio

44843

CHARLES E. MERRILL STUDIES

Under the General Editorship of
Matthew J. Bruccoli and Joseph Katz

Acknowledgement is made to Random House, Inc. for permission to quote from *Invisible Man,* by Ralph Ellison. Copyright © 1947, 1952 by Ralph Ellison.

ISBN: 0–675–09210–8

Library of Congress Catalog Number: 75–149740

1 2 3 4 5 6 7 8 9—79 78 77 76 75 74 73 72 71

Printed in the United States of America

Preface

Though Ralph Ellison characterized *Invisible Man* soon after its publication in 1952 as a "not quite fully achieved attempt at a major novel . . ." and two years later doubted that it would be around in twenty years because it was not "important," his first (and still only published) novel has established itself as one of the most widely read and generally admired American works of fiction published since the Second World War. Indeed, in 1965 it was judged by a *Book Week* poll of some 200 writers and critics to be "the most distinguished single work" published in the last 20 years. Whether because of its mythic substructure, its complexly ironic-comic perspective, its joy and energy of language, its social propheticness, or some other real or imagined virtue, *Invisible Man* has become a classic of our time, a book that repays investments of attention.

Among the best of the early responses—not all favorable, by the way—Steven Marcus's review instructively considers Ellison in conjunction with Richard Wright and James Baldwin in examining the way *Invisible Man* comes to terms with a distinctively Negro experience. Had space allowed, I would also have reprinted a review by R. W. B. Lewis (*Hudson Review*, VI [Spring 1953], 148) in which he argues that *Invisible Man* can be related to what he sees as the characteristically American arc of experience—"the adventures likely to befall a centerless individual en route through the flow and conflict of illusions towards some still undisclosed center." Thus, even at the beginning of its career, *Invisible Man* was understood to be specially pertinent to the history, condition and art of black Americans and, at the same time, to spring from and participate in broader themes and traditions.

In Part 2 Robert Bone assesses Ellison's career in general and the place of the novel in that career in particular. Bone convincingly shows how Ellison draws complexly on elements of his musical, literary and political heritage to deal with "these tangled themes: the relationship of Negro folk culture to American culture as a whole, and the responsibility of the Negro artist to his ethnic group." *

It is certainly true that any author must take his place among other critics of his own work; but obviously Ellison is in a unique position to offer information about his novel, his life, his sense of himself as a man and as an artist. Because Ellison has thought out loud so sensitively about these matters the reader is urged to consult some of the revealing interviews he has given, especially those readily available in *Shadow and Act*. In "The Art of Fiction," Part 3. of this volume, Ellison begins by denying that *Invisible Man* is an autobiographical work and goes on to discuss the sources and intentions of many key elements of the novel.

The fourth group of essays, as their titles clearly suggest, deal with specific themes, motifs and structural configurations. Vogler's provocative essay serves well as a bridge to those that follow. He opens with reflections on Ellison's relationship to traditions of literary, social and metaphysical protest and concludes with speculations on what Ellison's next novel might be like. But in between Vogler also deals with specific episodes, devices, images and symbols. In the essays in this section— particularly in Klein's—there is strong negative criticism as well as implicit and explicit adulation. This mixture of tough-minded objections to flaws and inconsistencies and shrewd perceptions of texture and structure are both test of and testimony to the novel's power to endure.

The single essay by Rodnon that concludes this collection is offered, aside from its other merits, in lieu of a reader's manual for *Invisible Man*. Students and teachers alike should find it instructive in pointing the way to future study, thought and writing. Together with the other pieces in this volume, it calls attention to

---

* Two other essays recommend themselves in this connection: Earl Rovit's "Ralph Ellison and the American Comic Tradition," *Wisconsin Studies in Contemporary Literature*, I (1960), 34–42, and Jonathan Baumbach's "Nightmare of a Native Son: Ralph Ellison's *Invisible Man*," from *The Landscape of Nightmare* (New York, 1965). The former emphasizes Ellison's "Americanness" of attitude and tone; the latter his relationship to themes and qualities of vision more nearly international in character.

the formal resonances of the novel and the complex sense of life it embodies. Finally, Rodnon's essay reminds us that after nearly two decades *Invisible Man* and its readers are far from having exhausted each other.

It is a pleasure to thank Ralph and Fanny Ellison for their interest and most helpful suggestions. Several other persons provided assistance of various kinds: Judy Bernheim carefully typed most of the manuscript, Robert Schildgen located several references, Cathy Flanagan skillfully oversaw the production of the volume and Valerie and Lann Gottesman did a number of chores with their usual cheerfulness and accuracy.

RG

For Gert and Pop

Contents

1. *Invisible Man* and the Negro Novel: A Review

Steven Marcus   2
    The American Negro in Search of Identity

2. A General Study: The Man and His Work

Robert A. Bone   16
    Ralph Ellison and the Uses of Imagination

3. Ellison on Ellison

Ralph Ellison   38
    The Art of Fiction: An Interview

4. Special Studies: Theme, Structure and Motif

Thomas Vogler   51
    Invisible Man: Somebody's Protest Novel

Marcus Klein   74
    Ralph Ellison's *Invisible Man*

William J. Schafer   89
    Ralph Ellison and the Birth of the Anti-Hero

Floyd R. Horowitz   100
    Ralph Ellison's Modern Version of Brer Bear and
    Brer Rabbit in *Invisible Man*

5. Suggestions for Study

Stewart Rodnon   109
    Ralph Ellison's *Invisible Man:* Six Tentative Approaches

1. A Review

Steven Marcus

The American Negro in Search of Identity
Three Novelists:
Richard Wright, Ralph
Ellison, James Baldwin

In picking up a novel about Negroes one feels almost as if the writer were starting from scratch—as if he were writing about people who have been deprived of culture and of coherent history. It is interesting that although there is much good English literature about India, English writing about Africa is often quite bad. Kipling, Forster, and Orwell wrote of India accepting the fact that the Indians had a culture, even when, like Orwell, they were intent on decrying it. In Africa, on the other hand, while there may have been the Negro race, there was for the European no recognizable culture; there was life, but no intelligible *way* of life, no immediately perceptible, coherent arrangement of rituals and institutions ordering the lives of its members, only an apparent vacuum of savagery and decay. This "vacuum," to be sure, was what interested the writer, who was therefore more inclined to yield to it than to look for the cultural reality that would have contradicted it; but too often it defeated him. The weaknesses of Conrad's *Heart of Darkness*, and even such less remarkable works as Buchan's *Prester John* and Joyce Cary's *Mister Johnson*, derive from the inexpressibility of that violent nothingness, which is supposed to be Africa.

With the exception of Mark Twain, this attitude towards Africa was carried over into American literature about Negroes: from Harriet Beecher Stowe to Faulkner, we have a record of the identification of blackness with sub-humanity of one form or another, whether perceived with civilized horror or sentimental identification. And Negro writers have themselves been infected with this attitude.

The error is understandable. After all, the novel itself has a history: it developed with the emergence of the modern consciousness of personality. African culture, with its essential stasis, its meager history, and the narrow possibilities its rituals afford, could hold

Reprinted from *Commentary*, XVI (1953), 456–63, by permission. Copyright © 1953 by the American Jewish Committee.

2

little interest for the novelist, who is concerned above all with the fate of the complex personality against a complex social background.

But American Negroes are no longer Africans, and the main problem for the serious writer dealing with them is to discover how Negro life in America operates to develop Negro personality. The two best novelists about race, Kipling and Faulkner, conceive of their job in terms of a problem in cultural miscegenation. Kim, for example, although he is white, has been raised as a Hindu, can pass for any kind of Indian, and is himself confused about who and what he is—an ambiguity which allows him to love and benefit from the two cultures which he straddles. Faulkner, although he encumbers himself with an unsatisfactory theological history about the Civil War, and although he often dehumanizes the Negroes all over again by allowing them only negative virtues ("they endured"), can create characters like Lucas Beauchamp and Joe Christmas, products of actual miscegenation, who are convincing in the dilemma of their identity. In these characters Faulkner resembles Kipling, and comes close to making some statement about the relation between two ways of life; ultimately, however, he does not do this, because to Faulkner also the Negro way of life has no essential organization: he can attribute little to it except passive or negative qualities, and he sees it too much as an unchanging element to play off against the fluidity of white society; Negro life for Faulkner is still "African," without culture.

Within the past year, three novels about Negroes by Negro writers have appeared. Ralph Ellison's *Invisible Man* and James Baldwin's *Go Tell It on the Mountain* are their first novels; Richard Wright's *The Outsider* is his second. All three are primarily concerned with the city Negro in the North, and all employ devices which are remarkably similar. Like Kipling and Faulkner they treat their subject as a problem in personal identity. And although it would be foolish to suppose that the existence of a Negro culture in America depends on whether or not it produced a literature, it can be said that insofar as these novelists create complex and genuine personalities in their writing, Negro culture in America has found self-consciousness and articulation.

Cross Damon, the hero of *The Outsider*, is a Chicago Negro, unhappily married, menaced by a pregnant mistress, and deeply in debt. Caught in a subway accident, he plants his identification papers on a badly mangled corpse and, having chosen a new personality for himself, devotes the remainder of his life to concealing

who he really is. This involves a flight to New York, joining the
Communist party, and several murders. In essence, *The Outsider*
is really another *Native Son*, and Cross Damon another Bigger
Thomas, no more. Like *Native Son*, *The Outsider* is full of inconsistencies and contradictions. Most of the book is very boring,
with long passages of didactic and quasi-philosophical prose. The
jargon of popularized psychology and existentialism washes over
the characters without clarifying them:

> But, above all, Dot had been to him a representation of a personal
> hunger which he had projected out of his heart on her, and the two
> of them—Dot and what she subjectively meant to him—had been
> something he had not been able to cope with with satisfaction to
> himself and honor to her. There had been no element of sadism in
> his love for Dot.

The theme of the book is flight: "... he was fleeing to escape
his identity, his old hateful consciousness." Cross Damon runs
away from everything—himself, his life, society, thought—everything, that is, except violence. In violence—much as Mr. Wright
tries to deny it—he finds his being. The story comes to life only
when Cross is meditating or performing some act of violence: "He
stepped upon the crushed body, feeling his shoes sinking into the
lifeless flesh and seeing blood bubbling from the woman's mouth
as his weight bore down on her breast." This impulse toward a
moment of supreme destruction and horror is typical of Mr.
Wright's vision. Invariably his heroes are swept into the dumb and
helpless backwashes of raging violence and sexuality—the conventional Negro hallmark and fate.

All through *The Outsider*, Mr. Wright keeps telling us that the
least important thing about his hero is that he is a Negro: "For
Cross had had no party, no myths, no tradition, no race, no soil,
no culture, and no ideas. ..." He is trying thus to portray modern
man in his existential loneliness—

> Cross had to discover what was good or evil through his own ac-
> tions, which were more exacting than the edicts of any God because
> it was he alone who had to bear the brunt of their consequences
> with a sense of absoluteness made intolerable by knowing that this
> life of his was all he had and would ever have.

—but in fact, instead of "universalizing" the Negro, he simply
denies the Negro's experience and reality. It is impossible that a

man should have "no race, no soil, no culture, and no ideas." In his self-conscious effort to turn his hero into a symbol of "modern man," Mr. Wright has simply reasserted that African "nothingness" which represented the failure of earlier writers to come into living relation with Negro life. Mr. Wright, it turns out, is unable to say anything at all about being a Negro except that to be a Negro is to be incoherent, and to do violence and murder. The point is not that violence and murder are absent from Negro life—I am not suggesting that Mr. Wright should have written a more "positive" novel—but that the figure of Cross Damon is not given enough reality to permit us an insight into these phenomena. Not by presenting a Negro murderer, but by denying in effect that the murderer is a Negro, Mr. Wright has again played into the hands of those who despise his people. Emptying his hero's life of all content—except that "existential" content which evades reality through the pretense of trying to grapple with it on its "deepest" level—he has left us with only the familiar old black chasm. From the question of identity Cross Damon makes a clean getaway; Mr. Wright leaves American Negro life as undiscovered and inarticulate as if he had never actually participated in it.

Ralph Ellison's *Invisible Man* is a basically comic work in the picaresque tradition, influenced especially by the novels of Louis-Ferdinand Céline. The hero of *Invisible Man* just happens to be a Negro, and everything he is and does includes ultimately the experience of all modern men. But this is not accomplished by abstraction; Mr. Ellison has managed to realize the fact of his hero's being a Negro in exactly the same way as 19th-century novelists realized their characters' being French or Russian or middle class: by making it the chief fact of their lives, something they take for granted and would not think of denying. Mr. Ellison displays an unapologetic relish for the concrete richness of Negro living—the tremendous variety of its speech, its music, its food, even its perversities.

Here are three random examples from the many kinds of Negro speech he transcribes:

A preacher at a Negro college:

Picture it, my young friends: The clouds of darkness all over the land, black folk and white folk full of fear and hate, wanting to go forward, but each fearful of the other. . . . All this . . . had been told and retold throughout the land, inspiring a humble but fast-rising people.

A West Indian African Nationalist:

Don't deny you'self! It took a billion gallons of black blood to make
you. Recognize you'self inside and you wan the kings among men!
A mahn knows he's a mahn when he got not'ing, when he's naked—
nobody have to tell him that. You six foot tall, mahn. You young
and intelligent. You black and beautiful—don't let 'em tell you different! You wasn't them t'ings you be dead, mahn. Dead! I'd have
killed you, mahn. Ras the Exhorter raised up his knife and tried to
do it, but he could not do it. Why don't you do it? I ask myself. I
will do it now, I say; but somet'ing tell me, "No, No. You might be
killing your black king!" And I say, yas, yas! So I accept your hu-
miliating ahction. Ras recognized your black possibilities, mahn.

A Harlem sharpster:

Me? I'm over on the side where some stud done broke in a store
and is selling cold beer out the window—Done gone in to business,
man; I was drinking me some Budweiser and digging the doings—
when here comes the cops up the street, riding like cowboys, man;
and when ole Ras-the-what's-his-name sees 'em he lets out a roar
like a lion and rears way back and starts shooting spurs into the
hoss's ass as fast as nickels falling in the subway at going-home
time—and gaawddam! that's when you ought to seen him! Say,
gimme a taste, there, fella.

Although this exploitation of his own milieu seems a simple
enough thing to expect of a novelist, the measure of Mr. Ellison's
achievement is apparent when we realize that he is the first Negro
to have done it convincingly. And, correlatively perhaps, his hero
is the only Negro in modern fiction who has no crippling desire to
be white. The precondition of Mr. Ellison's work is the well-
assimilated, conscious experience of Negro culture, not as indepen-
dent or entirely distinct, but as one of the many highly developed
sub-cultures that exist in America. The book offers innumerable
incidents and observations which demonstrate this; in fact,
Invisible Man impresses one as being perhaps overcrowded with
incident, leaving little room to turn around in. The formless, expan-
sive picaresque novel, however, is just the right thing for a novelist
who is in the act of discovering a culture. And in discovering this
culture, Mr. Ellison's hero begins to find out about the personality
he is seeking.

Where "the outsider" fled from his Negro identity, the "invisible
man" rushes toward it and is almost submerged in the plenitude
and diversity of Negro life. In a wonderfully comic chapter, the
hero, fleeing both from the hooligans of Ras, the African National-

ist, and from the Communists, disguises himself by putting on dark glasses and a hat. He is immediately mistaken by all Harlem for a character named Rinehart, who, it turns out, is an enigma himself, a man of many identities—a racketeer, a reverend, a philanthropist, a great lover. Everyone knows Rinehart, it seems, but nobody knows who he is; and as the hero, the "invisible man," makes this discovery, the comic absurdity of his position dawns on him, and he finds in the possibilities that exist in his Harlem world a richness he had never before supposed:

> Still, could he be all of them: Rine the runner and Rine the gambler and Rine the briber and Rine the lover and Rinehart the Reverend? Could he himself be both rind and heart.... His world was possibility and he knew it.... The world in which we lived was without boundaries. A vast seething, hot world of fluidity, and Rine the rascal was at home.... You could actually make yourself anew. The notion was frightening....

But if Mr. Ellison has appropriated all the secular culture of Harlem, he has not allowed it to vulgarize him; there are, in his book, no Rochesters or Bill Robinsons, nor, for that matter, Cross Damons, foisted upon us as the real thing. *Invisible Man* is, as far as I know, the first novel by a Negro to break away from the old, constrictive ideology; in Ras the Destroyer, Mr. Ellison has absorbed that myth as part of his drama, while through his comedy he has held it at arm's length where it cannot obscure the clarity of his view.

If Mr. Wright refused to consider the fact of being a Negro, and if Mr. Ellison, by assuming it, did not find it necessary to discuss it, James Baldwin has tried to define precisely what it is like. *Go Tell It on the Mountain* may be the most important novel yet written about the American Negro. *The Outsider* fled from Negro identity, *Invisible Man* toward it; *Go Tell It on the Mountain* is a book in which the characters move between two possible identities —identities which represent the limits to the possibilities of life as imposed by Negro culture. In Mr. Baldwin's novel, Negro culture is a different thing altogether from the vacuum of Mr. Wright's Harlem or the maelstrom of Mr. Ellison's. Mr. Wright has no ideas about the limits of culture, because he has hardly any sense of the concrete; and the main flaw in *Invisible Man*—as is seen in the prologue and epilogue—is that Mr. Ellison is unwilling to discover the specific limits to his ample experience. On the other hand, Mr. Baldwin's awareness of the outrageously narrow range of Negro life, and his insistence on its inflexibility, make the "question" of Negro culture, as we have considered it in relation to Mr. Wright and Mr. Ellison, almost irrelevant. Mr. Baldwin's concern with Negro culture is not so much to deny or discover it, but to present it in its pitifully tragic contradictions. His portrayal of Negro life demonstrates how the myth of African savagery is perpetuated among the Negroes themselves both by the condition of the Negro community in America and by the institution that affords their principal refuge from that savagery, religion.

John Grimes, the young hero of the novel, is an intelligent boy, sensitive to his intellectual abilities and his difference from other Negroes, and has resolved to revolt. "For he had made his decision. He would not be like his father, or his father's fathers. He would have another life." In Central Park he climbs a hill, and surveys from its eminence the spires of the city downtown—his future dominion:

> Before him, then, the slope stretched upward, and above it the brilliant sky, and beyond it, cloudy, and far away, he saw the skyline of New York. He did not know why, but there arose in him an exultation and a sense of power, and he ran up the hill like an engine, or a madman, willing to throw himself headlong into the city that glowed before him.... For it was his; the inhabitants of the city had told him it was his; he had but to run down, crying, and they would take him to their hearts and show him wonders his eyes had never seen.

This, he believes, will be his rich destiny, one that he may possess only if he sheds, like a butterfly shedding its cocoon, the world of his family, their life of fanatic religion, the culture of Harlem, of the Negroes.

But his dreams and desires are never to be fulfilled, for that evening at the "tarry service" of the violent Baptist sect of which his father is a deacon, John succumbs to his guilt and to his longings for reconciliation with his family, with his Negro-ness, and with God, and is seized by a religious convulsion. In submitting to it he chooses one of the two fates allowed the Negro. If he were to revolt, as so many in his family had done, the world would strike him down. If, on the other hand, he accepts the literal nothingness of what the world offers, and forfeits his hopes for a better life on earth, he will be accepting the burden of religion and of being a Negro. Suspended over the mouth of Hell, John sees the dreadful future that lies in store for him if he tries to escape what Mr. Baldwin conceives as the modern Negro's fate: the endurance of calamity, the renunciation of earthly pleasure, the acceptance of no fulfillment—the entire negative side of Christianity. John submits to the call of religion, subscribes to the doctrine of the Gospels, and is, as the book closes, reconciled to his condition.

And yet the lives of his parents are ironic and overwhelming evidence that he will find no rest or consummation even in this marginal way. His conversion, bringing in its wake a momentary breathing spell, a community with his family, and a rich, full sense of his being as a Negro, will sooner or later only aggravate his awareness of oppression, of the violent, gratuitous injustice done him by the world—and so will increase the intensity of his religious life, if it does not eventually destroy it. The life he moves toward as a result of his conversion is tyrannically restrictive, but it is the only "safe" one his culture extends. If John Grimes were to choose "sin"—that is, if he were to try to live the life of a normal American—he would not only be condemned by his religion, but would almost certainly be rejected by the larger culture he would be trying to enter and the society whose restrictions on Negro life set up the painful dualism beneath which he and the rest of the author's characters suffer.

There are two "mountains" in this book. When, at the end, John is "saved" and has begun his tortured ascent of the mountain of Holiness, we feel that the injustice of his condition is subsumed for the moment in the larger, impersonal justice of the novel—the strange justice of tragedy. This is his doom, and there is a rightness about it if only because it is inevitable. But we recall that other "mountain," the hill in Central Park from which John, at the beginning of the book, looked down beneath "the brilliant sky, and beyond it, cloudy and far away, he saw the skyline of New York." It is the same kind of elevation from which, I am sure Mr. Baldwin wants us to remember, Eugène de Rastignac, at the close of *Père Goriot*, surveys Paris. It is the prominence from which all the "young men from the provinces" catch their glimpse of the worlds they are to love and win. But for John Grimes there can be no winning; and when we realize this, that he can stand only on the mountain of Holiness, an otherworldly mountain made of bitterness and renunciation, a mountain where he finds his real identity, the poignancy of his earlier vision comes upon us with great force.

Exception may well be taken to the extremity of Mr. Baldwin's view. There is another kind of adjustment to the world that Ne-

groes can and do make—the sort, for example, that the hero of
Invisible Man manages. It may be argued, however, that a novel
like Mr. Baldwin's, which delineates its characters in terms of
tragic extremes, makes clearer and more possible, not to say more
urgent, that middle ground of adjustment so conspicuously absent
from its own domain. Mr. Baldwin has elsewhere trenchantly declared his antipathy to the kind of "protest novel" which ignores
the personality of the Negro; now he has written a novel which is
the strongest protest that can be made, because it intelligently
faces the complex dilemma of its characters.

What it is like to be a Negro is best comprehended in the stories
of the earlier lives of the members of John's family, which give to
John's religious upheaval a vitality and significance it otherwise
would not have. In all their experience there is one overarching
similarity:

> There was not, after all, a great difference between the world of the
> North and that of the South which [they] had fled; there was only
> this difference: the North promised more. And this similarity:
> what it promised it did not give, and what it gave, at length and
> grudgingly with one hand, it took back with the other.

The fundamental quality in the lives of these Negroes is frustration; every demand they make on life is rejected. It can be said
this is essentially true for all of us, but it is surely many times
truer for the Negroes. For us the larger world which limits our fulfillment and cuts down our demands is almost impersonal—it is
the world of nature, or of institutions so old and traditional that
they seem themselves almost natural—institutions whose sanc-
tions often appear as kindly in protecting us as they are malevolent
in denying our desires. But the Negro inhabits a universe that
extends at least the *chance* of fulfillment to everyone but himself.
He must work in the midst of wealth and status, but must live and
breed on the margins of society; at the same time he covets the
material and social felicities as much as anyone—indeed, more
than anyone, for since he has so little direct experience of them,
their value is magnified. It is not surprising, then, that the exces-
siveness of the Negroes' sense of sin, so bound up in their desires
for the pleasures of the world, is in direct proportion to their distance from the social, material abundance it contains.

Although *Go Tell It on the Mountain* is meticulously planned,
and every episode is organic to the governing conception, it is not

primarily a novel of delicate relations, subtle qualifications, and minutely discriminated personalities. There is instead a force above the characters and their relations—adequately realized though they are—which creates an impression of terrible uniformity and strangeness. One of the best things this novel does is to capture all the uniqueness, foreignness, and exoticism of Negro life. Like an anthropologist, Mr. Baldwin shows us these people under the aspect of homogeneity; their individual lives represent their collective fate. Misled by our impulses to atone for the oppression of the Negroes, we have too often denied them a character distinct from our own—that is, we have reversed the myth of Africa. In his intense, narrow vision (a vision not less true because of its limitation), Mr. Baldwin shows the basic separateness of his people without making them depersonalized savages.

Mr. Baldwin's fiction is much like that of another very talented contemporary, Saul Bellow. In his second novel, *The Victim*, Mr. Bellow set out to do something very like what Mr. Baldwin had done—to define just what it is like to be an assimilated American Jew. The main character in *The Victim* is also suspended between two possibilities of existence in very much the same way as Mr. Baldwin's Negroes are—although the Jewish possibilities are different from the Negro possibilities. What it is like to be an American Jew today is a precarious thing for a novel to concern itself with, of course, since Jewish culture has undergone a degree of assimilation that the Negro community has hardly begun to approach. Thus, one of the main difficulties in writing about the modern American Jew comes from having to reckon with his "cosmopolitanism." This is not the case for the Negro writer; his people have not had much access to those respectable, functional positions in society through which the Jews long ago began to acquire sophistication and bring their identity into contact with the world outside the ghetto. The chief difficulty for a Negro writer is just the reverse: he must continually salvage from the strangeness and narrowness of his community something to link him to Western man and open up that common ground of culture with the white man which will save him from the final deadliness of his isolation. The point of the parallel between Jew and Negro lies in just this: that where the Jew is becoming more and more anxious to rediscover that by now elusive quality which makes him Jewish, the Negro is becoming more and more anxious to discover his kinship with the white race and with human history—for it is surely true that the Negroes themselves believe, however unwillingly, in their own "savagery." The Jew, it might be said, is hunting for his lost separateness—the Negro, for his unbestowed universality.

Go Tell It on the Mountain is not a "religious novel" in any of the ways we have recently come to expect; it is not interested in religious dogma, nor in the disparagement of it. Religion is rather the vehicle of this novel, its means of expression, and not its primary concern. Nevertheless, Mr. Baldwin has given religion that organic function it rarely possesses in the modern novel. The Negroes are perhaps the only people today in whose culture the literalness of Christianity has been preserved, and who can really assert that they are like the Jews in Egypt or the Christians in Rome. Mr. Baldwin's ability to make the fact of religion relevant and central to the lives of his characters is a testimony to his intelligent use of an existing tradition. Religion in this book is *the* institution of Negro society, and thus—just as is the case with secular Negro life in *Invisible Man*—demands no special treatment or sophistical justification to insure its reality. Yet Mr. Baldwin does not, I think, make the error of claiming more for the religion of these Negroes than it can show—that religion offers coherence to otherwise chaotic lives and permits them to go on living without destroying themselves. It does not cure their ailments, or stop their sinning, or change their personalities; while preserving their hold on life it also kills much of their response to it. There is none of the generosity in their religion characteristic of Christianity at its highest, and it is one of the most disturbing things about this brilliant novel that it extends neither to the characters nor to the reader that generosity characteristic of the best novels—the kind of generosity exemplified, for example, in George Eliot's portrayal of Bulstrode in *Middlemarch*, Dostoevsky's Verhovensky in *The Possessed*, or James's Kate Croy in *The Wings of the Dove*. The ability of these novelists to force us into sympathy with really wicked characters is a species of detachment still beyond Mr. Baldwin's powers. His treatment of Gabriel, John's father (who is, significantly, not his real father), seems to me to bear traces of mere vindictiveness. This is a very serious flaw, since the working out of a relation between John and his father is central to the main theme of the book—John's discovery of himself.

It must be said also that as the episodes of *Go Tell It on the Mountain* unfold, a rather nasty kind of irony begins to assert itself. Although each event in the novel conveys both a religious import and an awareness that life is being sacrificed for religion's sake, Mr. Baldwin's desire to give both points of view has led him in some places to substitute a poised indecisiveness for his usual superb impersonality. Unfortunately, the full compassion that John's fate should elicit sometimes resides merely on the surface of the prose, in formal gestures:

> And the dust made him cough and retch; in his turning the center of the whole earth shifted, making of space a sheer void and a mockery of order, and balance, and time. Nothing remained: all was swallowed up in chaos. And: *Is this it?* John's terrified soul inquired—*What is it?*—to no purpose, receiving no answer. Only the ironic voice insisted once more that he rise from that filthy floor if he did not want to become like all the other niggers.

There are two kinds of rhetoric at work in this passage. The first is inflated—"swallowed up in chaos," etc.—and is supposed to convey John's torment. The "ironic voice" of the last sentence, on the other hand, represents Mr. Baldwin's attempt to balance or deflate the extravagance of his hero's religious experience. This is characteristic of almost every passage in the section that deals with the conversion. Clearly, however, neither term is adequately presented, nor are the two impulses they represent reconciled. The clichés in the first part of the passage, and the uneasiness in "filthy" and "nigger," are sufficient evidence for the unsureness of touch which blemishes the last section of the book. The truth is that Mr. Baldwin is not sure of what he wants to say, finally, and he disguises this uncertainty in an affected distance from his material. This indecisiveness, with its compensating impulse toward neatness, seems to me a real fault. It leads to a certain falseness of tone and withholding of commitment—one might almost say of Mr. Baldwin's own identity—that constrict the novel and divest it of moral backbone. This is very much like that faulty irony in Hardy's novels, which eats away at the stature of the characters, forcing them to fit an idea which dominates the novelist's mind; T. S. Eliot's comment on Hardy applies equally to Mr. Baldwin: "He will leave nothing to nature, but will always be giving one last turn of the screw himself."

In considering these three novels and their backgrounds, certain things become apparent.

The Negro remains, for the most part, still locked inside his own world, looking toward the white world outside and longing to be there; and it is his deep hatred of his own condition, even of his own body, that the Negro novelist must deal with. As long as he despises his existence, the Negro will try to escape it; and Mr. Ellison and Mr. Baldwin demonstrate how the Negro's attempt to cut the traces of his personality can be turned to account—a reconciliation beyond Mr. Wright's comprehension. It is the destiny of the Negro to be surrounded by a world which he knows is better and more beautiful than the one he must inhabit; but by constantly doubting his identity, and by manipulating it, he tries to arrive somehow closer to that world outside.

Without a doubt the Negroes in America have a kind of life that is fully capable of producing good literature; it has taken a long time to develop—much longer than most of us, since we are Americans, believed necessary—and no doubt was there long before any of us bothered to think about it. The fact of that life is as much demonstrated by Mr. Wright's disastrous attempt to deny it as it is by its turning out two first-rate writers like Mr. Ellison and Mr. Baldwin, whose novels, in almost complete opposition at all points, are both valid and suggestive in relation to the same problem. These novels show us that today as much as ever a writer of genius and intelligence can master and re-interpret the world around him, and does not invariably need aristocratic courts or ruined abbies or some impossible kind of society to spoon-feed him into creativity.

And indeed, the failure of Mr. Wright and the success of Mr. Ellison and Mr. Baldwin suggest again that—for the novelist and for ourselves—men are often most human where they are most different, and in their diversity is the key to their ultimate likeness.

2. General Studies: The Man and His Work

Robert Bone

Ralph Ellison and the Uses of Imagination

We live only in one place at one time, but far from being bound by it, only through it do we realize our freedom. We do not have to abandon our familiar and known to achieve distinction; rather in that place, if only we make ourselves sufficiently aware of it, do we join with others in other places.

WILLIAM CARLOS WILLIAMS

Some fourteen years ago an unknown writer, no longer young, published a first novel and, to no one's astonishment more than his own, won the National Fiction Award for 1952. There, suddenly, was the novel, and it spoke eloquently enough, but who was the author of *Invisible Man?* We knew only that the curve of his life was a parabola, moving from Oklahoma City to New York by way of Alabama. In the intervening years we have had some fleeting glimpses of the man and his ideas: the acceptance speech itself, an occasional interview, a fragment of his work in progress. We might have noticed his music criticism in the *Saturday Review* or the recent exchange with Irving Howe in *The New Leader.* But basically the man behind the mask remained invisible.

Now, with the publication of *Shadow and Act,** this remarkable man emerges, at least in silhouette, to the public view. The book contains most of Ellison's essays, from the beginning of his literary career to the present. There are seven apprentice pieces, written in the Forties, which reflect the author's social and political concerns, and seven essays on jazz and the blues, which appeared principally in the late Fifties. There are three interviews of the *Paris Review* genre, and three first-rate essays on literary topics. Along the way, we learn a good deal about the author and the forces that have shaped his sense of life.

The formative years in Oklahoma City are sketched in some detail. Ellison was born in 1914, just seven years after Oklahoma was admitted to the Union. In the early days, his adopted grand-

---

Reprinted from *Anger and Beyond* (New York: Harper & Row, Publishers, 1966), pp. 86–111, by permission of the author. Copyright © 1969 by Robert Bone.

* New York: Random House, 1964.

16

father had led a group of settlers from Tennessee to the Oklahoma Territory. Containing such elements, the Negro community of Oklahoma City developed more a Western than a Southern tone. Race relations, like all social relations, were more fluid than in established communities. Frontier attitudes persisted well into the present century, and Ellison was raised in a tradition of aggressiveness and love of freedom. He is proud of his frontier heritage, and to it may be traced his fierce individualism and his sense of possibility.

Oklahoma City was a boomtown in the postwar years—a swirling vortex of social styles and human types. There were many masks which an imaginative adolescent might try on:

> Gamblers and scholars, jazz musicians and scientists, Negro cowboys and soldiers from the Spanish-American and First World Wars, movie stars and stunt men, figures from the Italian Renaissance and literature, both classical and popular, were combined with the special virtues of some local bootlegger, the eloquence of some Negro preacher, the strength and grace of some local athlete, the ruthlessness of some businessman-physician, the elegance in dress and manners of some headwaiter or hotel doorman.*

If there was no local writer for a model, there was access to a rich oral literature in the churches, schoolyards, barbershops, and cotton-picking camps. And there was a curious double exposure to the exacting habits of artistic discipline. Through one of the ironies of segregation, the Negro school system placed particular stress on training in classical music. Ellison took up the trumpet at the age of eight and studied four years of harmony in high school. Meanwhile he was exposed to the driving beat of Southwestern jazz, of which Kansas City, Dallas, and Oklahoma City were acknowledged centers. From his boyhood onward, he was caught up in that creative tension between the folk and classical traditions which has remained the richest resource of his art.

In 1933 Ellison enrolled at Tuskegee Institute to study composition under William Dawson, the Negro conductor and composer. In his sophomore year, however, he came upon a copy of *The Waste Land*, and the long transition from trumpet to typewriter had begun. He read widely in American fiction and, initially scorning the moderns, developed a lifelong devotion to the nineteenth-

---

* *Shadow and Act*, pp. xv–xvi.

century masters. On coming to New York in 1936 he met Richard Wright, who introduced him on the one hand to the prefaces of Conrad and the letters of Dostoevski, and on the other to the orbit of the Communist party. One evening he accompanied Wright to a fund-raising affair for the Spanish Loyalists, where he met both Malraux and Leadbelly for the first time. It was a notable occasion, symbolic of the times and of the cross-pressures exerted from the first upon his art.

From these cross-pressures Ellison derived his most enduring themes. How could he interpret and extend, define and yet elaborate upon the folk culture of the American Negro and, at the same time, assimilate the most advanced techniques of modern literature? How could he affirm his dedication to the cause of Negro freedom without succumbing to the stridencies of protest fiction, without relinquishing his complex sense of life? In *Shadow and Act*, Ellison returns again and again to these tangled themes: the relationship of Negro folk culture to American culture as a whole, and the responsibility of the Negro artist to his ethnic group.

As instrumentalist and composer, Ellison had faced these issues for the better part of two decades. When he began to write, it was natural for him to draw upon his musical experience for guidelines and perspectives. Not that his approach to writing is merely an extension of an earlier approach to jazz and the blues; they tend, in fact, to reinforce each other. But his experience with jazz was formative; it left a permanent mark upon his style. His controlling metaphors are musical, and if we are to grasp his thought, we must trace his language to its source. There, in the world of Louis Armstrong and Charlie Parker, Bessie Smith and Jimmy Rushing, we may discover the foundations of Ellison's aesthetic.

Music

The essence of jazz is group improvisation. Its most impressive effects are achieved, according to Ellison, when a delicate balance is maintained between the individual performer and the group. The form itself, consisting of a series of solo "breaks" within a framework of standard chord progressions, encourages this balance. "Each true jazz moment," Ellison explains, "springs from a contest in which each artist challenges all the rest; each solo flight, or improvisation, represents (like the successive canvases of a painter) a definition of his identity: as individual, as member of the collectivity, and as a link in the chain of tradition." "True jazz," he concludes, "is an art of individual assertion within and against the group."

Here is a working model for the Negro writer. By balancing conflicting claims upon his art, he can solve his deepest problems of divided loyalty. As an artist with a special function to perform within the Negro group, the writer must be careful to preserve his individuality. He must learn to operate "within and against the group," allowing neither claim to cancel out the other. Similarly on the cultural plane, where the Negro's group identity is at stake. Here the writer can affirm whatever is uniquely Negro in his background while insisting precisely on the American quality of his experience. "The point of our struggle," writes Ellison, "is to be both Negro and American and to bring about that condition in American society in which this would be possible."

Closely related to the question of individual and group identity is that of personal and traditional styles. Every jazz musician must strike a balance between tradition and experimentation, for "jazz finds its very life in an endless improvisation upon traditional materials." It follows that no jazzman is free to repudiate the past. The jam session, where he must display a knowledge of traditional techniques, will see to that. He must master "the intonations, the mute work, manipulation of timbre, the body of traditional styles" before he can presume to speak in his own voice. The path, in short, to self-expression lies through what is given, what has gone before.

As an American Negro writer, Ellison inherits a double obligation to the past. He must become familiar with a folk tradition which is his alone, and with a wider literary culture which he shares. Moreover, he must strive in both dimensions for a proper blend of past and present, given and improvised. In describing his response to his folk tradition, Ellison draws a parallel to the work of Picasso: "Why, he's the greatest wrestler with forms and techniques of them all. Just the same, he's never abandoned the old symbolic forms of Spanish art: the guitar, the bull, daggers, women, shawls, veils, mirrors." Similarly, Ellison appropriates folkloristic elements from Negro culture, embroiders on them, adapts them to his literary aims, and lifts them to the level of a conscious art.

In the wider context of American literature, the same principles apply. Consider Ellison's experimental idiom. Not since Jean Toomer has a Negro novelist been so inventive of new forms, new language, new technical devices. And yet none has been so deeply immersed in the American literary past. As Ellison struggles toward the realization of a personal style, he is *improvising* on the achievement of our nineteenth-century masters. It is this body of writing, he insists, "to which I was most attached and through which . . . I would find my own voice, and to which I was challenged, by way of achieving myself, to make some small contribution, and to whose composite picture of reality I was obligated to offer some necessary modifications."

Still a third balance must be struck between constraint and spontaneity, discipline and freedom. For the jazzman owes his freedom to the confident possession of technique. From his own struggles with the trumpet, Ellison learned how much the wild ecstatic moment depends on patient hours of practice and rehearsal. Freedom, he perceived, is never absolute, but rooted in its opposite. The game is not to cast off all restraint but to achieve, within the arbitrary limits of a musical tradition, a transcendent freedom. Jazz taught Ellison a respect for limits, even as it revealed the possibility of overcoming limits through technique. It was the blues, however, that taught him to discern in this paradox an emblem of the human condition.

The blues arise out of a tension between circumstance and possibility. The grim reality that gives them birth bespeaks the limits and restrictions, the barriers and thwartings, which the universe opposes to the human will. But the tough response that is the blues bespeaks a moral courage, a spiritual freedom, a sense of human possibility, which more than balances the scales. In Ellison's words, "The blues is an art of ambiguity, an assertion of the irrepressibly human over all circumstance whether created by others or by one's own human failings. They are the only consistent art in the United States which constantly reminds us of our limitations while encouraging us to see how far we can actually go."

The blues begin with personal disaster. They speak of flooded farmlands and blighted crops, of love betrayed and lovers parted, of the black man's poverty and the white man's justice. But what matters is the human response to these events. For the blues are a poetic confrontation of reality. They are a form of spiritual discipline, a means of transcending the painful conditions with which they deal. The crucial feature of the blues response is the margin of freedom it proclaims. To call them an art of ambiguity is to assert that no man is entirely the victim of circumstance. Within limits, there is always choice and will. Thinking of this inner freedom, Ellison speaks of "the secular existentialism of the blues."

This sense of possibility lies at the center of Ellison's art. It explains his devotion to his craft, for what is technique but another name for possibility? It explains his attitude toward protest fiction, for the propaganda novel, in portraying the Negro primarily as victim, gives more weight to circumstance than possibility. Ellison's is a more plastic sensibility. His heroes are not victims but adventurers. They journey toward the possible in all ignorance of accepted limits. In the course of their travels, they shed their illusions and come to terms with reality. They are, in short, picaresque heroes, full of "rash efforts, quixotic gestures, hopeful testings of the complexity of the known and the given."

If circumstance often enough elicits tears, possibility may release a saving laughter. This blend of emotion, mixed in some ancient cauldron of the human spirit, is characteristic of the blues. It is a lyricism better sampled than described. Note in Ellison's example how the painful humiliation of the bird is controlled, or absorbed, or even converted into triumph by a kind of grudging laughter:

> Oh they picked poor robin clean
> They picked poor robin clean
> They tied poor robin to a stump
> Lord, they picked all the feathers
> Round from robin's rump
> Oh they picked poor robin clean.

The blues have nothing to do with the consolations of philosophy. They are a means of neutralizing one emotion with another, in the same way that alkalies can neutralize an acid stomach. For the American Negro, they are a means of prophylaxis, a specific for the prevention of spiritual ulcers. It is not a question of laughing away one's troubles in any superficial sense, but of gazing steadily at pain while perceiving its comic aspect. Ellison regards this tragicomic sensibility as the most precious feature of his Negro heritage. From it stems his lyrical intensity and the complex interplay of tragic and comic elements which is the distinguishing mark of his fiction.

If the blues are primarily an expression of personal emotion, they also serve a group need. Perhaps the point can best be made through a comparison with gospel singing. When Mahalia Jackson sings in church, she performs a ritual function. Her music serves "to prepare the congregation for the minister's message, to make it receptive to the spirit and, with effects of voice and rhythm, to evoke a shared community of experience." Similarly in the secular context of the blues. When Jimmy Rushing presided over a Saturday night dance in Oklahoma City, he was acting as the leader of a public rite: "It was when Jimmy's voice began to soar with the spirit of the blues that the dancers—and the musicians—achieved that feeling of communion which was the true meaning of the public jazz dance."

We are dealing here with substitute rituals. During an epoch which has witnessed the widespread breakdown of traditional religious forms, Ellison finds in jazz and the blues, as Hemingway found in the bullfight, a code of conduct and a ceremonial framework for his art. "True novels," he insists, "arise out of an impulse to celebrate human life and therefore are ritualistic and ceremonial at their core." Ellison perceives, in short, the priestly office of the modern artist and assumes the role of celebrant in his own work. Like the blues singer, he is motivated by an impulse to restore to others a sense of the wholeness of their lives.

Finally, specific features of Ellison's literary style may be traced to his musical background. His fondness for paradox and ambiguity, for example, derives from the blues: "There is a mystery in the whiteness of blackness, the innocence of evil and the evil of innocence, though being initiates Negroes express the joke of it in the blues." The changing styles of *Invisible Man* (from naturalism to expressionism to surrealism, as Ellison describes the sequence) are based on the principle of modulation. Chord progressions in jazz are called "changes"; they correspond in speed and abruptness to Ellison's sense of American reality, the swift flow of sound and sudden changes of key suggesting the fluidity and discontinuity of American life.

Literature

Let us now turn from Ellison's musical to his literary heritage. We must begin with the picaresque novel and attempt to explain why this form, which first appeared in Renaissance Spain, should be revived by a contemporary Negro novelist. We must then consider Ellison's affinity for the American transcendentalists, in light of his commitment to the picaresque. Finally, we must examine in some detail two devices that are central to his art.

The picaresque novel emerged toward the end of the feudal and the beginning of the bourgeois epoch. Its characteristic hero, part

rogue and part outlaw, transcended all established norms of conduct and violated all ideas of social hierarchy. For with the breakdown of static social relations, a testing of personal limits, a bold
confrontation with the new and untried became necessary. Hence
the picaresque journey, no longer a religious quest or pilgrimage
but a journey toward experience, adventure, personal freedom. It
was the journey of the bourgeois soul toward possibility, toward a
freedom possessed by neither serf nor lord under the old regime.

It can hardly be an accident that *Invisible Man* and *The Adventures of Augie March* should win the National Fiction Award
within two years of one another. Nor that Ellison and Bellow
should each acknowledge a major debt to Twain. For *Huckleberry
Finn* is the last great picaresque novel to be written by a white
Anglo-Saxon American. The genre has been abandoned to the
Negro and the Jew who, two generations from slavery or the
shtetl, experiences for the first time and in full force what Ellison
calls the magical fluidity of American life. A century after Hawthorne wrote *The Scarlet Letter,* our minority groups are re-enact-
ing the central drama of that novel: the break with the institutions
and authorities of the past and the emergence into an epoch of
personal freedom and individual moral responsibility.

Ellison's revival of the picaresque reflects his group's belated
access to the basic conditions of bourgeois existence. These consist
economically of the freedom to rise and psychologically of "the
right and opportunity to dilate, deepen, and enrich sensibility."
The Southern Negro who is taught from childhood to "know his
place" is denied these basic freedoms. He is deprived of individuality as thoroughly as any serf: "The pre-individualistic black community discourages individuality out of self-defense. . . . Within the
ambit of the black family this takes the form of training the child
away from curiosity and adventure, against reaching out for those
activities lying beyond the borders."

The Great Migration of the Negro masses from Southern farm
to Northern city was picaresque in character. In terms of Negro
personality, it was like uncorking a bottle of champagne. Traditionally the journey has been made by railroad, and it is no accident that the blues are associated with freight yards, quick get-
aways and long journeys in "a side door Pullman car." No accident
either that Ellison should emphasize his own wanderings: "To
attempt to express that American experience which has carried one
back and forth and up and down the land and across, and across
again the great river, from freight train to Pullman car, from con-

tact with slavery to contact with the world of advanced scholarship, art and science, is simply to burst such neatly understated forms of the novel asunder."

The bursting forth of Negro personality from the fixed boundaries of Southern life is Ellison's essential theme. And it is this, at bottom, that attracts him to the transcendentalists. For what was the central theme of Thoreau, Emerson and Whitman, if not the journeying forth of the soul? These writers were celebrating their emancipation from the Custom House, from the moral and political authority of old Europe. Their romantic individualism was a response to the new conditions created by the Revolution, conditions calling for *self*-government in both the political and moral sphere. Their passion for personal freedom, moreover, was balanced by a sense of personal responsibility for the future of democracy.

Ellison's debt to transcendentalism is manifold, but what is not acknowledged can easily be surmised. He is named, to begin with, for Ralph Waldo Emerson. In this connection he mentions two specific influences: the "Concord Hymn" and "Self-Reliance." The poem presumably inspires him with its willingness to die that one's children may be free; the essay, as we shall see, governs his attitude toward Negro culture. He admires Thoreau, plainly enough, for his stand on civil disobedience and his militant defense of John Brown. Whitman he finds congenial, for such poems as "The Open Road" and "Passage to India" are squarely in the picaresque tradition.

In broader terms, it may be said that Ellison's ontology derives from transcendentalism. One senses in his work an unseen reality behind the surfaces of things. Hence his fascination with guises and disguises, with the con man and the trickster. Hence the felt dichotomy between visible and invisible, public and private, actual and fictive modes of reality. His experience as a Negro no doubt reinforces his ironic awareness of "the joke that always lies between appearance and reality," and turns him toward an inner world that lies beyond the reach of insult or oppression. This world may be approached by means of the imagination; it is revealed during the transcendent moment in jazz or the epiphany in literature. *Transcend* is thus a crucial word in Ellison's aesthetic.

Above all, Ellison admires the transcendentalists for their active democratic faith. They were concerned not only with the slavery question but with the wider implications of cultural pluralism, with the mystery of the one and the many. To these writers, the national motto, *e pluribus unum*, was a serious philosophical concern. Emerson discerned a cosmic model for American democracy in the relationship of soul to Oversoul. Whitman, however, made the classic formulation:

> One's self I sing, a simple separate person,
> Yet utter the word Democracy, the word En-Masse.

Ellison reveals, in his choice of ancestors, the depth of his commitment to American ideals. When he describes jazz as "that embodiment of a superior democracy in which each individual cultivated his uniqueness and yet did not clash with his neighbors," he is affirming the central values of American civilization.

It remains to place Ellison in his twentieth-century tradition. What is involved is a rejection of the naturalistic novel and the philosophical assumptions on which it rests. From Ellison's allusions to certain of his contemporaries—to Stein and Hemingway, Joyce and Faulkner, Eliot and Yeats—one idea emerges with persistent force: *Man is the creator of his own reality.* If a culture shapes its artists, the converse is equally the case: "The American novel is in this sense a conquest of the frontier; as it describes our experience, it creates it." This turn toward subjectivity, this transcendence of determinism, this insistence on an existential freedom, is crucial to Ellison's conception of the artist. It finds concrete expression in his work through the devices of masking and naming.

Masking has its origin in the psychological circumstances of Southern life: "In the South the sensibilities of both blacks and whites are inhibited by the rigidly defined environment. For the Negro there is relative safety as long as the impulse toward individuality is suppressed." As soon, however, as this forbidden impulse seeks expression, an intolerable anxiety is aroused. Threatened by his own unfolding personality as much as by the whites, the Negro learns to camouflage, to dissimulate, to retreat behind a protective mask. There is magic in it: the mask is a means of warding off the vengeance of the gods.

Consider the jazz solo, one of the few means of self-expression permitted to the southern Negro. Precisely because it is a solo, and the musician must go it alone, it represents potential danger. Ellison writes of certain jazz musicians: "While playing in ensemble, they carried themselves like college professors or high church deacons; when soloing they donned the comic mask." Louis Armstrong, as Ellison reminds us, has raised masking to the level of a fine art. Musical trickster, con man with a cornet, Elizabethan clown, "he takes liberties with kings, queens, and presidents." In a later development, the bearded mask of the bopster appeared, frankly expressive of hostility, rudeness and contempt. It is a pose which still finds favor among certain Negro writers of the younger generation.

In his own prose, Ellison employs various masking devices, including understatement, irony, *double-entendre* and calculated ambiguity. There is something deliberately elusive in his style, something secret and taunting, some instinctive avoidance of explicit statement which is close in spirit to the blues. His fascination with masquerade gives us two memorable characters in *Invisible Man:* the narrator's grandfather, whose mask of meekness conceals a stubborn resistance to white supremacy, and Rinehart, whom Ellison describes as "an American virtuoso of identity who thrives on chaos and swift change." A master of disguise, Rinehart survives by manipulating the illusions of society, much in the tradition of Melville's Confidence Man, Twain's Duke and Dauphin and Mann's Felix Krull.

Masking, which begins as a defensive gesture, becomes in Ellison's hands a means of altering reality. For if reality is a process of becoming, that process can be partially controlled through manipulation of a ritual object or mask. "Masking," Ellison remarks, "is a play upon possibility," and possibility is precisely the domain of art. To clarify the matter he summons Yeats, a man not ignorant of masks: "If we cannot imagine ourselves as different from what we are and assume the second self, we cannot impose a discipline upon ourselves, though we may accept one from others. Active virtue, as distinct from the passive acceptance of a current code, is the wearing of a mask." Yeats is speaking of morality, of active virtue, but the function of the artist is implicit in his words. Before pursuing the point, however, we must come to terms with a second feature of Ellison's art.

Naming likewise has its origin in negation, in the white man's hypocritical denial of his kinship ties. For the African slaves received from their Christian masters not only European names but a massive infusion of European blood, under circumstances so brutal and degrading as to have been virtually expunged from the national consciousness. At once guilty and proud, the white man has resorted to a systematic *misnaming* in an effort to obscure his crime. Thus the use of the matronymic to conceal the slave's paternity. Thus the insulting epithets which deny not merely kinship but humanity. In some obscene rite of exorcism, the white man says "nigger" when he should say "cousin." And yet the family names persist as symbols of that hidden truth, that broken connection which will have to be restored before the nation, sick from the denial of reality, can regain its mental health.

Having been misnamed by others, the American Negro has attempted from the first to define himself. This persistent effort at self-definition is the animating principle of Negro culture. The earliest appearance of Negro folklore, for example, "announced the Negro's willingness to trust his own experience, his own sensibilities as to the definition of reality, rather than allow his masters to define these crucial matters for him." Similarly with musical expression: the jazzman who rejects classical technique is affirming his right to define himself in sound. Cultural autonomy, to Ellison, is an elementary act of self-reliance. We have listened too long, he seems to say, to the courtly Muses of white America. "Our names, being the gift of others, must be made our own."

For personal as well as historical reasons, Ellison is fascinated by the distinction between one's given and achieved identity. Named for a famous poet, it was half a lifetime before he could define, let alone accept, the burden of his given name. Acknowledging in retrospect the prescience of his father, he speaks of "the suggestive power of names and the magic involved in naming." We are dealing here with the ritual use of language, with the pressure which language can exert upon reality. This is the special province of the poet, and, broadly speaking, Ellison claims it as his own. He regards the novel as an act of ritual naming; the novelist, as a "moralist-designate" who *names* the central moral issues of his time.

"The poet," writes Ralph Waldo Emerson, "is the Namer or Language-maker." As such, he is the custodian of his language and the guarantor of its integrity. In performance of this function, Ellison has discovered that the language of contemporary America is in certain ways corrupt. "With all deliberate speed," for example, does not mean what it seems to mean when uttered by the Supreme Court of the United States. He proposes a rectification of the language and, therefore, of the nation's moral vision. For accurate naming is the writer's first responsibility: "In the myth, God gave man the task of naming the objects of the world; thus one of the functions of the poet is to insist upon a correspondence between words and ever-changing reality, between ideals and actualities."

As with naming, so with the image-making function as a whole. The artist, or image-maker, is guardian of the national iconography. And since the power of images for good or evil is immense, he bears an awesome responsibility. If his images are false, if there is no bridge between portrayal and event, no correspondence between the shadow and the act, then the emotional life of the nation is to that extent distorted, and its daily conduct is rendered ineffectual or even pathological. This is the effect of the anti-Negro stereotype, whether in song or statuary, novel or advertising copy, comic strip or film. Images, being ritual objects, or masks, may be manipulated by those who have a stake in the preservation of caste lines. What is required is a rectification of the nation's icons, a squaring of the shadow and the act.

Nor can this be accomplished through the use of counter-stereotypes. Protest fiction, by portraying sociological types, holds its readers at a distance from the human person. But the problem is precisely one of identification. To identify, in the psychological sense, is to become one with. For this process to occur between white reader and Negro character, the writer must break through the outer crust of racial conflict to the inner core of common humanity. He must evoke, by his imaginative power, an act of "painful identification." To succeed requires the utmost in emotional maturity, craftsmanship and skill. For what the artist undertakes, in the last analysis, is the rectification of the human heart.

Politics

If Ellison had remained a jazz musician, he might have been spared a series of political attacks upon his art. No one would have complained, if he had spoken in a jazz idiom, that his riffs were lacking in protest content. No one would have accused him, as he blew up there on the bandstand, of abandoning a posture of clenched militancy. For it is not-expected of a Negro jazzman that, like the first trumpet in the Dodger Fan Club, he should sit in the stands during every civil-rights contest and play at appropriate moments, "Da da da datta da: Charge!" So long as he refuses to play for segregated audiences, accepts no gigs from the State Department and does an occasional benefit for SNCC, he is allowed to go about the very difficult business of interpreting Negro experience in sound.

Not so with the Negro novelist, who works in the medium of words. For words have a variety of uses, political exhortation being one. The ideologists, therefore, move in. The question of militancy is raised, bearing not on the novelist's conduct as a citizen or political man but precisely on his creative work, his function as an artist. To those who feel above all else the urgency of the Negro's political struggle, it is not enough that a writer demonstrate his solidarity; he must enlist his image-making powers in the service of the cause. Since no writer who understands the proper uses of imagination can acquiesce in this perversion of his talent, he must prepare to walk that lonesome valley during much of his career, and to accept a good deal of abuse from those who do not recognize the value of his art.

It was predictable enough, given the rising tempo of the civil-rights struggle, that Ellison should be under pressure from the political activists. The Freedom Movement, like all great movements of social liberation, is lacking neither in demagogues nor Philistines. But that so sophisticated a critic and humane a man as Irving Howe should join the attack is scandalous. In an article called "Black Boys and Native Sons," * Howe takes Baldwin and Ellison to task for abandoning the "rasping outbursts," "black anger," and "clenched militancy" of Richard Wright. While he sees some signs of hope in Baldwin's recent work, he plainly regards Ellison as unregenerate. Howe's essay prompted a reply from Ellison, and the result was a sharp exchange in *The New Leader*.†

One's chief impression of this debate is that the antagonists are arguing at cross-purposes. They shout at one another, but little or no dialogue occurs. Howe's original piece is a monument to tactlessness, and Ellison is understandably provoked into a sometimes angry response. It is a bad show all around, and the issues deserve to be aired in a calmer atmosphere. It is not my intent to mediate, however, for in my opinion Howe is overwhelmingly in the wrong. Nor do I wish to repeat Ellison's arguments which—tone aside— make most of the essential points. I should like rather to explore the philosophical foundations of the controversy. If my argument seems elementary, it is best that we proceed with caution, since, plainly, each of the contestants feels threatened by the other at the center of his being.

---

* *Dissent*, Autumn, 1963.

† Dec. 9, 1963, and Feb. 3, 1964. Howe's original piece has been reprinted in *A World More Attractive* (New York: Horizon Press, 1963); Ellison's rejoinder appears in *Shadow and Act* under the title "The World and the Jug."

Let me begin with a parable. Imagine a Negro writer in the late 1950's (I choose the period advisedly, for Howe describes it as a conservative decade) attempting to decide on a subject for a novel. He has before him two projects, each based on the life of a Dodger baseball hero. The one—call it the Jackie Robinson story —is alive with racial drama: the first Negro ball-player to make the big time, the insults from the stands, the spikings by opposing players, the mixed reception from his teammates. The other—call it the Roy Campanella story—concerns an athlete who, at the height of his career, spun his car around a curve one icy morning and spent the rest of his life in a wheelchair. Within a year or two his wife divorced him, she, too, a victim of her human frailty.

Suppose, for purposes of argument, that our writer chose to tell the second story. Would that choice suggest to Howe that he was running from reality, the reality of the sharpened spikes? Or is it possible that the Campanella story also contains a reality sufficiently sharp? Nor is there a refusal to confront injustice, for the theme of the second story would have to be injustice on a cosmic scale. Perhaps Howe would attempt a political explanation of our writer's choice. He might propose that during the militant decade of the Thirties such a writer would have turned at once to Jackie Robinson, but that out of his "dependence on the postwar *Zeitgeist*" he turned instead to a subject that was safe. But perhaps these political categories are beside the point. Perhaps our writer chose as he did simply because he felt in that story a deeper sense of human life.

Not all human suffering is racial in origin, that is our initial point. Being Negro, unfortunately, does not release one from the common burdens of humanity. It is for this reason that the blues singer so often deals with other than his racial woes. And it is to this dimension of human, as opposed to racial, pain that Howe gives insufficient attention. Ultimately, Ellison and Howe are divided over the *locus* of human suffering. One stresses man's position in society; the other, his position in the universe at large.

At issue is a crucial distinction between remediable and irremediable evil. The first, roughly speaking, is the domain of politics and science; the second, of art and religion. One's sense of tragedy is linked to one's perception of irremediable evil. What we have, therefore, in the Howe-Ellison exchange, is a confrontation between Howe's political optimism and Ellison's tragic sensibility. Howe, who still believes in Progress, concentrates on the evil that can be changed to the neglect of that which must be borne.

To the white liberal, racial injustice is a remediable evil. The Negro, however, experiences it in both modes simultaneously. In historical time, things are no doubt getting better, but in one's own lifetime, white oppression is a bitter fact to which one must adjust. The Negro, as Ellison points out, must live with and suffer under the present reality even as he works to change it. Entirely apart from the Movement, he must concern himself with the strategies and techniques of personal survival. It is precisely with this necessity of Negro life that Ellison's art is engaged.

Because of Howe's bias toward remediable evil, it is difficult for him to understand redemptive suffering. Speaking of Richard Wright, he remarks, "He examines the life of the Negroes and judges it without charity or idyllic compensation—for he already knows, in his heart and his bones, that to be oppressed means to lose out on human possibilities." This half-truth, it seems to me, dehumanizes the Negro by depriving him of his human triumph over pain. For as Ellison insists, Negro life is not only a burden but a discipline. Is it idyllic to suggest that Campanella's experience as a Negro might have prepared him in some way for coping with his accident? Was it in any way relevant? Was it, in short, an emotional resource?

If one attends primarily to remediable evil, one may be tempted to make larger claims for politics than history can justify. One may end by making politics the touchstone of a man's humanity: "In response to Baldwin and Ellison, Wright would have said ... that only through struggle could men with black skins, and for that matter, all the oppressed of the world, achieve their humanity." Perhaps the question of humanity is after all more complex. It would be impertinent to remind Howe, who is a close student of the subject, that in recent Russian history many struggled and were brutalized thereby. But the memoirs of Victor Serge suggest to me that even in the midst of revolution the artist has a special function to perform: to remind the revolution of its human ends.

It will be clear, I trust, that I am speaking out of no hostility to the Freedom Movement or to politics as such. I am arguing not for the abandonment of militancy but for the autonomy of art. There is no need for literature and politics to be at odds. It is only when the aesthete approaches politics as if it were a poem, or when the political activist approaches the poem as if it were a leaflet, that the trouble starts. Phrases like "only through struggle" urge the subordination of art to politics. We must stifle these imperialistic impulses and foster a climate of mutual respect Emerson distinguishes between the Doer and the Sayer, and refuses to honor one at the expense of the other. "Homer's words," he observes, "are as costly to Homer as Agamemnon's victories are to Agamemnon."

And I would add that Homer's words are as valuable as Agamemnon's victories *to the Greeks*. For I am arguing throughout for the social value of art. When Howe touches on this aspect of the question, he tries invariably to pre-empt all social value for his own position. Ellison, he charges, is pursuing the essentially antisocial goal of "personal realization," while Wright is fulfilling his responsibility to the Negro community. It is a false dichotomy. The Negro writer, who is surely not free of social responsibility, must yet discharge it *in his own fashion*, which is not the way of politics but art; not the lecture platform but the novel and the poem. Without repudiating his sense of obligation to the group, Ellison has tried to express it through services which only the imagination can perform.

What is at issue is the role of the imagination in that complex process which we call civilization. The visionary power, the power of naming, the power of revealing a people to itself are not to be despised. If those who can command these powers are diverted from their proper task, who will celebrate the values of the group, who create those myths and legends, those communal rites which alone endow the life of any group with meaning? These gifts are no less precious to a people (and if you like, no more) than those of personal charisma, theoretical analysis and political organization which are the special province of the revolutionary. Let us therefore give the imaginative faculty its due, concede its social value and respect its unique contribution to the process of becoming man.

Culture

At least as important as Ellison's defense of the imagination is his contribution to a theory of American Negro culture. Previous work in the field, whether by Negro or white intellectuals, has stressed the autonomous character of Negro culture, viewing it as an alien or exotic tributary to the mainstream of American life. Ellison proposes a more integrated view. Negro folk culture, to his way of thinking, is an indestructible monument to the national past. Embodying as it does three centuries of American history, it is a bittersweet reminder of what we were and are as a people. Far from being isolated from the mainstream, it marks the channel where the river runs deepest to the sea.

Given the complex interplay of culture and personality, race and social class that shapes the lives of American Negroes, some degree of theoretical clarity, some modicum of sophistication in these matters is essential. Not only racial strategies but one's own sanity and peace of mind are at stake. For every American Negro responds, at some level of his being, to two apparently disjunctive cultural traditions. If this can be shown to be an arbitrary division, false to the realities of American history, not only will the personal tensions ease but the Freedom Movement will be seen in new perspective. Integration will now appear as a mutual attempt, by American whites as well as Negroes, to restore a splintered culture to a state of wholeness.

The problem of dual identity is particularly acute for members of the Negro middle class. Suspended between two cultural traditions, each with its own claims and loyalties, the educated Negro has been caught on the horns of a dilemma. To identify closely with the life-style of the white middle class has generally led to a rejection of Negro folk culture. Conversely, to identify closely with the life-style of the Negro masses has implied a disaffection with the dominant values of American civilization. This conflicting pattern of identification and rejection has produced two broad currents of thought and feeling which I have elsewhere called assimilationism and Negro nationalism. Let me describe them briefly, for purposes of contrast with Ellison's point of view.

Assimilationism is a natural response to the experience of upward mobility. As the Negro middle class becomes differentiated from the masses by virtue of income, education and social status, it looks back upon its origins with embarrassment and shame. Negro folk culture, this rising middle class would argue, is the creation of an illiterate peasantry. It is vulgar and often shocking, permeated with the smell of poverty, reminiscent of our degradation and our pain. However well it may attest to what we were, it contains nothing of enduring value for us or for our children. On the contrary, it is a major obstacle to integration. The white middle class will accept us only to the extent that we become like them. It is therefore necessary to expunge every trace of "Negroness" from our behavior.

To these arguments Ellison would counterpose the richness of his folk tradition. He insists upon the relevance of folk experience to the conditions of modern urban life and, more important still, to the condition of being man. The assimilationist demands that in the name of integration the Negro self be put to death. But Ellison regards this proposal as a projection of self-hatred. To integrate means to make whole, not to lop off or mutilate; to federate as equals, not to merge and disappear. Anything else is a denial not only of one's racial identity but of one's national identity as well. For slavery really happened on American soil, and it has made us both, Negro and white alike, what we are today.

Negro nationalism is a natural response to the experience of rejection. Rebuffed by the whites, the Negro nationalist rebuffs in turn. Rejecting the white man's civilization as thoroughly corrupt, visibly in decay and hopelessly compromised by its oppression of the blacks, he asks in anger and despair, "Why should we integrate into a burning house?" From this mood of separatism and alienation flows his attitude toward the folk culture. For here is a system of values to oppose to those of the white middle class. All that is distinctive in Negro life is thus exalted as a matter of racial pride. Traditionally, this point of view has been fortified by some sort of African mystique, the current version being the concept of *Négritude.*

Here Ellison would counter with the richness of the dominant tradition. European civilization, of which he is a part, cannot be written off so lightly. Emerson and Einstein, Mozart and Michelangelo, Jefferson and Joyce are part of his tradition, and he has paid for them in blood. He is not about to bargain them away in exchange for *Négritude.* The Negro nationalist demands that for the sake of injured pride the Western self be put to death. But if the injury is real, the remedy is disastrous. What is separatism but the sulking of a rejected child? The American Negro, after all, is no stranger to the affairs of this nation. Nor can he stand aside from its appointed destiny. For if the house burns, one thing is certain: the American Negro will not escape the conflagration.

Assimilationism and Negro nationalism both involve a maiming of the self, an unnecessary loss. Why not combine the best of both traditions? Between these opposite and symmetrical errors, Ellison steers a steady course. On the one hand, he wants in: no one, white or colored, will persuade him that he is an outsider. Talk about the mainstream! He's been swimming in it since 1619. On the other hand, he is not about to trade in his tested techniques of survival on some white man's vague promise: "Be like us and we will accept you, maybe." When he comes in, he brings his chitlins with him. If, in the process, he transforms America into a nation of chitlin eaters, so much the better for our ethnic cooking.

While assimilationism and Negro nationalism make opposite evaluations of Negro folk culture, they both regard it as in some sense un-American. To all such formulations Ellison objects that

they abstract distinctive Negro qualities from the concrete circumstances of American life. The American Negro *is* different from
his white countrymen, but American history and that alone has
made him so. Any serious attempt to understand these differences
will, therefore, lead, by a thousand devious paths, across the tracks
to white America. Always there is a connection, however hidden;
always a link, however brutally severed. It follows that "any viable
theory of Negro American culture obligates us to fashion a more
adequate theory of American culture as a whole."

To this end, Ellison offers what might be called some Notes
toward a Redefinition of American Culture. There is a gross
distortion, he suggests, in America's self-image. It begins with the
white man's artificial attempt to isolate himself from Negro life.
But Negro life is not sealed off hermetically from the historical
process. On the contrary, it is the most authentic expression of
that process as it has actually unfolded on the North American
continent. Ellison argues, in effect, that the life-style of the Negro
ghetto is *more* American than the so-called standard American
culture of white suburbia because the latter, in the very impulse
that gave it birth, denies a vital dimension of American experience.
There is no possibility, he warns of escaping from the past. What
is required is that we bring our distorted image of ourselves into
line with the historical reality.

Paradoxically, what is most distinctive in Negro life is often
most American. Jazz, for example, is not simply Negro music, but
the definitive rendering of American experience in sound. Similarly
with folklore: "In spilling out his heart's blood in his contest with
the machine, John Henry was asserting a national value as well
as a Negro value." Where do we turn for the truth about American
slavery: to Negro spirituals or the songs of Stephen Collins Foster?
Why is the current slang of American teen-agers drawn from the
speech of the Negro ghetto? Why the persistent vogue for Negro
dance forms, unless we have been growing, from Charleston to
Watusi, steadily less inhibited as a nation?

American culture is still in process of becoming. It is not a
finished form, a house that one day will be rented out to Negroes.
On the contrary, in the process of racial integration the culture
will be radically transformed. This transformation will amount to
a correction of perspective. By degrees, the white man's truncated
version of American reality will be enlarged. The American eye will
be retrained to see sights hitherto ignored or, if seen, misconstrued
for venal ends. Connections formerly obscure will now be plain;

the essential oneness of American civilization will emerge. Ultimately Americans will develop a new image of themselves as a nation.

"I was taken very early," Ellison remarks, "with a passion to link together all I loved within the Negro community and all those things I felt in the world which lay beyond." This passion is the driving force of his career. It can be felt in his response to jazz as well as his approach to fiction. It accounts, moreover, for his views on politics and art. For the linking together which he has in mind can barely begin in courthouse and in workshop, neighborhood and school. It must be consummated in some inner realm, where all men meet on common ground. Such are the links that Ellison would forge, the new reality he would create, the shattered psyche of the nation that he would make whole.

3. Ellison on Ellison

The Art of Fiction: An Interview

RALPH ELLISON: Let me say right now that my book [*Invisible Man*] is not an autobiographical work.

INTERVIEWERS (ALFRED CHESTER, VILMA HOWARD): You weren't thrown out of school like the boy in your novel?

ELLISON: No. Though, like him, I went from one job to another.

INTERVIEWERS: Why did you give up music and begin writing?

ELLISON: I didn't give up music, but I became interested in writing through incessant reading. In 1935 I discovered Eliot's *The Waste Land*, which moved and intrigued me but defied my powers of analysis—such as they were—and I wondered why I had never read anything of equal intensity and sensibility by an American Negro writer. Later on, in New York, I read a poem by Richard Wright, who, as luck would have it, came to town the next week. He was editing a magazine called *New Challenge* and asked me to try a book review of E. Waters Turpin's *These Low Grounds*. On the basis of this review Wright suggested that I try a short story, which I did. I tried to use my knowledge of riding freight trains. He liked the story well enough to accept it and it got as far as the galley proofs when it was bumped from the issue because there was too much material. Just after that the magazine failed.

INTERVIEWERS: But you went on writing—

ELLISON: With difficulty, because this was the Recession of 1937. I went to Dayton, Ohio, where my brother and I hunted and sold game to earn a living. At night I practiced writing and studied Joyce, Dostoievsky, Stein and Hemingway. Especially Hemingway; I read him to learn his sentence structure and how to organize a story. I guess many young writers were doing this, but I also used his description of hunting when I went into the fields the next day. I had been hunting since I was eleven but no one had broken down the process of wing-shooting for me and it was from reading Hemingway that I learned to lead a bird. When he describes something in print, believe him; believe him even when he describes the process of art in terms of baseball or boxing; he's been there.

INTERVIEWERS: Were you affected by the social realism of the period?

ELLISON: I was seeking to learn and social realism was a highly regarded theory, though I didn't think too much of the so-called proletarian fiction even when I was most impressed by Marxism. I was intrigued by Malraux, who at that time was being claimed by the Communists. I noticed, however, that whenever the heroes of *Man's Fate* [1] regarded their condition during moments of heightened self-consciousness, their thinking was something other than Marxist. Actually they were more profoundly intellectual than their real-life counterparts. Of course, Malraux was more of a humanist than most of the Marxist writers of that period—and also much more of an artist. He was the artist-revolutionary rather than a politician when he wrote *Man's Fate*, and the book lives not because of a political position embraced at the time, but because of its larger concern with the tragic struggle of humanity. Most of the social realists of the period were concerned less with tragedy than with injustice. I wasn't, and am not, primarily concerned with injustice, but with art.

INTERVIEWERS: Then you consider your novel a purely literary work as opposed to one in the tradition of social protest.

ELLISON: Now mind! I recognize no dichotomy between art and protest. Dostoievsky's *Notes from Underground* is, among other things, a protest against the limitations of nineteenth-century rationalism; *Don Quixote, Man's Fate, Oedipus Rex, The Trial*—all these embody protest, even against the limitation of human life itself. If social protest is antitheatrical to art, what then shall we make of Goya, Dickens and Twain? One hears a lot of complaints about the so-called "protest novel, especially when written by Negroes; but it seems to me that the critics could more accurately complain about their lack of craftsmanship and their provincialism.

INTERVIEWERS: But isn't it going to be difficult for the Negro writer to escape provincialism when his literature is concerned with a minority?

ELLISON: All novels are about certain minorities: the individual is a minority. The universal in the novel—and isn't that what we're all clamoring for these days?—is reached only through the depiction of the specific circumstance.

INTERVIEWERS: But still, how is the Negro writer, in terms of

---

[1] La Condition Humaine.

what is expected of him by critics and readers, going to escape his particular need for social protest and reach the "universal" you speak of?

ELLISON: If the Negro, or any other writer, is going to do what is expected of him, he's lost the battle before he takes the field. I suspect that all the agony that goes into writing is borne precisely because the writer longs for acceptance—but it must be acceptance on his own terms. Perhaps, though, this thing cuts both ways: the Negro novelist draws his blackness too tightly around him when he sits down to write—that's what the anti-protest critics believe— but perhaps the white reader draws his whiteness around himself when he sits down to read. He doesn't want to identify himself with Negro characters in terms of our immediate racial and social situation though on the deeper human level, identification can become compelling when the situation is revealed artistically. The white reader doesn't want to get too close, not even in an imaginary re-creation of society. Negro writers have felt this and it has led to much of our failure.

Too many books by Negro writers are addressed to a white audience. By doing this the authors run the risk of limiting themselves to the audience's presumptions of what a Negro is or should be; the tendency is to become involved in polemics, to plead the Negro's humanity. You know, many white people question that humanity but I don't think that Negroes can afford to indulge in such a false issue. For us the question should be, What are the specific *forms* of that humanity, and what in our background is worth preserving or abandoning. The clue to this can be found in folklore, which offers the first drawings of any group's character. It preserves mainly those situations which have repeated themselves again and again in the history of any given group. It describes those rites, manners, customs, and so forth, which insure the good life, or destroy it; and it describes those boundaries of feeling, thought and action which that particular group has found to be the limitation of the human condition. It projects this wisdom in symbols which express the group's will to survive; it embodies those values by which the group lives and dies. These drawings may be crude but they are nonetheless profound in that they represent the group's attempt to humanize the world. It's no accident that great literature, the products of individual artists, is erected upon this humble base. The hero of Dostoievsky's *Notes from Underground* and the hero of Gogol's *The Overcoat* appear in their rudimentary forms far back in Russian folklore. French literature has never ceased exploring the nature of the Frenchman . . . Or take Picasso—

INTERVIEWERS: How does Picasso fit into all this?

ELLISON: Why, he's the greatest wrestler with forms and techniques of them all. Just the same he's never abandoned the old symbolic forms of Spanish art: the guitar, the bull, daggers, women, shawls, veils, mirrors. Such symbols serve a dual function: they allow the artist to speak of complex experiences and to annihilate time with simple lines and curves; and they allow the viewer an orientation, both emotional and associative, which goes so deep that a total culture may resound in a simple rhythm, an image. It has been said that Escudero could recapitulate the history and spirit of the Spanish dance with a simple arabesque of his fingers.

INTERVIEWERS: But these are examples from homogeneous cultures. How representative of the American nation would you say Negro folklore is?

ELLISON: The history of the American Negro is a most intimate part of American history. Through the very process of slavery came the building of the United States. Negro folklore, evolving within a larger culture which regarded it as inferior, was an especially courageous expression. It announced the Negro's willingness to trust his own experience, his own sensibilities as to the definition of reality, rather than allow his masters to define these crucial matters for him. His experience is that of America and the West, and is as rich a body of experience as one would find anywhere. We can view it narrowly as something exotic, folksy or "low-down," or we may identify ourselves with it and recognize it as an important segment of the larger American experience—not lying at the bottom of it, but intertwined, diffused in its very texture. I can't take this lightly or be impressed by those who cannot see its importance; it is important to *me*. One ironic witness to the beauty and the universality of this art is the fact that the descendants of the very men who enslaved us can now sing the spirituals and find in the singing an exultation of their own humanity. Just take a look at some of the slave songs, blues, folk ballads; their possibilities for the writer are infinitely suggestive. Some of them have named human situations so well that a whole corps of writers could not exhaust their universality. For instance, here's an old slave verse:

> *Ole Aunt Dinah, she's just like me*
> *She work so hard she want to be free*
> *But old Aunt Dinah's gittin' kinda ole*
> *She's afraid to go to Canada on account of the cold.*

Ole Uncle Jack, now he's a mighty "good nigger"
You tell him that you want to be free for a fac'
Next thin you know they done stripped the skin
    off your back.

Now old Uncle Ned, he want to be free
He found his way north by the moss on the tree
He cross that river floating in a tub
The patateroller [2] *give him a mighty close rub.*

It's crude, but in it you have three universal attitudes toward the problem of freedom. You can refine it and sketch in the psychological subtleties and historical and philosophical allusions, action and what not, but I don't think its basic definition can be exhausted. Perhaps some genius could do as much with it as Mann has done with the Joseph story.

INTERVIEWERS: Can you give us an example of the use of folklore in your own novel?

ELLISON: Well, there are certain themes, symbols and images which are based on folk material. For example, there is the old saying amongst Negroes: if you're black, stay back; if you're brown, stick around; if you're white, you're right. And there is the joke Negroes tell on themselves about their being so black they can't be seen in the dark. In my book this sort of thing was merged with the meanings which blackness and light have long had in Western mythology: evil and goodness, ignorance and knowledge, and so on. In my novel the narrator's development is one through blackness to light; that is, from ignorance to enlightenment: invisibility. He leaves the South and goes North; this, as you will notice in reading Negro folktales, is always the road to freedom—the movement upward. You have the same thing again when he leaves his underground cave for the open.

It took me a long time to learn how to adapt such examples of myth into my work—also ritual. The use of ritual is equally a vital part of the creative process. I learned a few things from Eliot, Joyce and Hemingway, but not how to adapt them. When I started writing, I knew that in both *The Waste Land* and *Ulysses* ancient myth and ritual were used to give form and significance to the material; but it took me a few years to realize that the myths and rites which we find functioning in our everyday lives could be used

---

[2] Patroller.

in the same way. In my first attempt at a novel—which I was unable to complete—I began by trying to manipulate the simple structural unities of *beginning, middle* and *end,* but when I attempted to deal with the psychological strata—the images, symbols and emotional configurations—of the experience at hand, I discovered that the unities were simply cool points of stability on which one could suspend the narrative line—but beneath the surface of apparently rational human relationships, there seethed a chaos before which I was helpless. People rationalize what they shun or are incapable of dealing with; these superstitions and their rationalizations become ritual as they govern behavior. The rituals become social forms, and it is one of the functions of the artist to recognize them and raise them to the level of art.

I don't know whether I'm getting this over or not. Let's put it this way: Take the "Battle Royal" passage in my novel, where the boys are blindfolded and forced to fight each other for the amusement of the white observers. This is a vital part of behavior pattern in the South, which both Negroes and whites thoughtlessly accept. It is a ritual in preservation of caste lines, a keeping of taboo to appease the gods and ward off bad luck. It is also the initiation ritual to which all greenhorns are subjected. This passage which states what Negroes will see I did not have to invent; the patterns were already there in society, so that all I had to do was present them in a broader context of meaning. In any society there are many rituals of situation which, for the most part, go unquestioned. They can be simple or elaborate, but they are the connective tissue between the work of art and the audience.

INTERVIEWERS: Do you think a reader unacquainted with this folklore can properly understand your work?

ELLISON: Yes, I think so. It's like jazz; there's no inherent problem which prohibits understanding but the assumptions brought to it. We don't all dig Shakespeare uniformly, or even *Little Red Riding Hood.* The understanding of art depends finally upon one's willingness to extend one's humanity and one's knowledge of human life. I noticed, incidentally, that the Germans, having no special caste assumptions concerning American Negroes, dealt with my work simply as a novel. I think the Americans will come to view it that way in twenty years—if it's around that long.

INTERVIEWERS: Don't you think it will be?

ELLISON: I doubt it. It's not an important novel. I failed of eloquence, and many of the immediate issues are rapidly fading away.

If it does last, it will be simply because there are things going on in its depth that are of more permanent interest than on its surface. I hope so, anyway.

INTERVIEWERS: Have the critics given you any constructive help in your writing, or changed in any way your aims in fiction?

ELLISON: No, except that I have a better idea of how the critics react, of what they see and fail to see, of how their sense of life differs with mine and mine with theirs. In some instances they were nice for the wrong reasons. In the United States—and I don't want this to sound like an apology for my own failures—some reviewers did not see what was before them because of this nonsense about protest.

INTERVIEWERS: Did the critics change your view of yourself as a writer?

ELLISON: I can't say that they did. I've been seeing by my own candle too long for that. The critics did give me a sharper sense of a larger audience, yes; and some convinced me that they were willing to judge me in terms of my writing rather than in terms of my racial identity. But there is one widely syndicated critical bankrupt who made liberal noises during the thirties and has been frightened ever since. He attacked my book as a "literary race riot." By and large, the critics and readers gave me an affirmed sense of my identity as a writer. You might know this within yourself, but to have it affirmed by others is of utmost importance. Writing is, after all, a form of communication.

INTERVIEWER: When did you begin *Invisible Man?*

ELLISON: In the summer of 1945. I had returned from the sea, ill, with advice to get some rest. Part of my illness was due, no doubt, to the fact that I had not been able to write a novel for which I'd received a Rosenwald Fellowship the previous winter. So on a farm in Vermont where I was reading *The Hero* by Lord Raglan and speculating on the nature of Negro leadership in the United States, I wrote the first paragraph of *Invisible Man*, and was soon involved in the struggle of creating the novel.

INTERVIEWERS: How long did it take you to write it?

ELLISON: Five years, with one year out for a short novel which was unsatisfactory, ill-conceived and never submitted for publication.

INTERVIEWERS: Did you have everything thought out before you began to write *Invisible Man?*

ELLISON: The symbols and their connections were known to me. I began it with a chart of the three-part division. It was a conceptual frame with most of the ideas and some incidents indicated. The three parts represent the narrator's movement from, using Kenneth Burke's terms, purpose to passion to perception. These three major sections are built up of smaller units of three which mark the course of the action and which depend for their development upon what I hoped was a consistent and developing motivation. However, you'll note that the maximum insight on the hero's part isn't reached until the final section. After all, it's a novel about innocence and human error, a struggle through illusion to reality. Each section begins with a sheet of paper; each piece of paper is exchanged for another and contains a definition of his identity, or the social role he is to play as defined for him by others. But all say essentially the same thing, "Keep this nigger boy running." Before he could have some voice in his own destiny he had to discard these old identities and illusions; his enlightenment couldn't come until then. Once he recognizes the hole of darkness into which these papers put him, he has to burn them. That's the plan and the intention; whether I achieved this is something else.

INTERVIEWERS: Would you say that the search for identity is primarily an American theme?

ELLISON: It is *the* American theme. The nature of our society is such that we are prevented from knowing who we are. It is still a young society, and this is an integral part of its development.

INTERVIEWERS: A common criticism of "first novels" is that the central incident is either omitted or weak. *Invisible Man* seems to suffer here; shouldn't we have been present at the scenes which are the dividing lines in the book—namely, when the Brotherhood organization moves the narrator downtown, then back uptown?

ELLISON: I think you missed the point. The major flaw in the hero's character is his unquestioning willingness to do what is required of him by others as a way to success, and this was the specific form of his "innocence." He goes where he is told to go; he does what he is told to do; he does not even choose his Brotherhood name. It is chosen for him and he accepts it. He has accepted party discipline and thus cannot be present at the scene since it is not the will of the Brotherhood leaders. What is important is not the scene but his failure to question their decision. There is also the fact that no single person can be everywhere at once, nor can a single consciousness be aware of all the nuances of a large social action. What happens uptown while he is downtown is part of his darkness, both symbolic and actual. No, I don't feel that any vital scenes have been left out.

INTERVIEWERS: Why did you find it necessary to shift styles throughout the book, particularly in the Prologue and Epilogue?

ELLISON: The Prologue was written afterwards, really—in terms of a shift in the hero's point of view. I wanted to throw the reader off balance—make him accept certain non-naturalistic effects. It was really a memoir written underground, and I wanted a foreshadowing through which I hoped the reader would view the actions which took place in the main body of the book. For another thing, the styles of life presented are different. In the South, where he was trying to fit into a traditional pattern and where his sense of certainty had not yet been challenged, I felt a more naturalistic treatment was adequate. The college Trustee's speech to the students is really an echo of a certain kind of Southern rhetoric and I enjoyed trying to re-create it. As the hero passes from the South to the North, from the relatively stable to the swiftly changing, his sense of certainty is lost and the style becomes expressionistic. Later on during his fall from grace in the Brotherhood it becomes somewhat surrealistic. The styles try to express both his state of consciousness and the state of society. The Epilogue was necessary to complete the action begun when he set out to write his memoirs.

INTERVIEWERS: After four hundred pages you still felt the Epilogue was necessary?

ELLISON: Yes. Look at it this way. The book is a series of reversals. It is the portrait of the artist as a rabble-rouser, thus the various mediums of expression. In the Epilogue the hero discovers what he had not discovered throughout the book: you have to make your own decisions; you have to think for yourself. The hero comes up from underground because the act of writing and thinking necessitated it. He could not stay down there.

INTERVIEWERS: You say that the book is "a series of reversals." It seemed to us that this was a weakness, that it was built on a series of provocative situations which were canceled by the calling up of conventional emotions—

ELLISON: I don't quite see what you mean.

INTERVIEWERS: Well, for one thing, you begin with a provocative situation of the American Negro's status in society. The responsibility for this is that of the white American citizen; that's where the guilt lies. Then you cancel it by introducing the Communist Party, or the Brotherhood, so that the reader tends to say to himself: "Ah, they're the guilty ones. They're the ones who mistreat him; not us."

ELLISON: I think that's a case of misreading. And I didn't

identify the Brotherhood as the C.P., but since you do I'll remind
you that they, too, are white. The hero's invisibility is not a matter
of being seen, but a refusal to run the risk of his own humanity,
which involves guilt. This is not an attack upon white society: It is
what the hero refuses to do in each section which leads to further
action. He must assert and achieve his own humanity; he cannot
run with the pack and do this—this is the reason for all the reversals. The Epilogue is the most final reversal of all; therefore it
is a necessary statement.

INTERVIEWERS: And the love affairs—or almost love affairs—

ELLISON: (*Laughing*) I'm glad you put it that way. The point is
that when thrown into a situation which he thinks he wants, the
hero is sometimes thrown at a loss; he doesn't know how to act.
After he had made his speech about the Place of the Woman in
Our Society, for example, and was approached by one of the women
in the audience, he thought she wanted to talk about the Brotherhood and found that she wanted to talk about brother-*and-
sisterhood*. Look, didn't you find the book at all *funny?* I felt that
such a man as this character would have been incapable of a love
affair; it would have been inconsistent with his personality.

INTERVIEWERS: Do you have any difficulty controlling your characters? E. M. Forster says that he sometimes finds a character
running away with him.

ELLISON: No, because I find that a sense of the ritual understruc-
ture of the fiction helps to guide the creation of characters. Action
is the thing. We are what we do and do not do. The problem for
me is to get from A to B to C. My anxiety about transitions greatly
prolonged the writing of my book. The naturalists stick to case
histories and sociology and are willing to compete with the camera
and the tape recorder. I despise concreteness in writing, but when
reality is deranged in fiction, one must worry about the seams.

INTERVIEWERS: Do you have any difficulty turning real characters into fiction?

ELLISON: Real characters are just a limitation. It's like turning
your own life into fiction: you have to be hindered by chronology
and fact. A number of the characters just jumped out, like Rinehart and Ras.

INTERVIEWERS: Isn't Ras based on Marcus Garvey? [3]

ELLISON: No. In 1950 my wife and I were staying at a vacation

[3] Marcus Garvey, Negro nationalist and founder of a "Back to Africa" movement in the U.S. during the early 1900s.

spot where we met some white liberals who thought the best way
to be friendly was to tell us what it was like to be Negro. I got mad
at hearing this from people who otherwise seemed very intelligent.
I had already sketched Ras but the passion of his statement came
out after I went upstairs that night feeling that we needed to have
this thing out once and for all and get it done with; then we could
go on living like people and individuals. No conscious reference to
Garvey is intended

INTERVIEWERS: What about Rinehart? Is he related to Rinehart
in the blues tradition, or Django Rheinhardt, the jazz musician?

ELLISON: There is a peculiar set of circumstances connected
with my choice of that name. My old Oklahoma friend, Jimmy
Rushing, the blues singer, used to sing one with a refrain that went:

> *Rinehart, Rinehart,*
> *It's so lonesome up here*
> *On Beacon Hill...*

which haunted me, and as I was thinking of a character who was
a master of disguise, of coincidence, this name with its suggestion
of inner and outer came into my mind. Later I learned that it was
a call used by Harvard students when they prepared to riot, a call
to chaos. Which is very interesting, because it is not long after
Rinehart appears in my novel that the riot breaks out in Harlem.
Rinehart is my name for the personification of chaos. He is also
intended to represent America and change. He has lived so long
with chaos that he knows how to manipulate it. It is the old theme
of *The Confidence Man*. He is a figure in a country with no solid
past or stable class lines; therefore he is able to move about easily
from one to the other. (*He pauses, thoughtfully*)

You know, I'm still thinking of your question about the use of
Negro experience as material for fiction. One function of serious
literature is to deal with the moral core of a given society. Well,
in the United States the Negro and his status have always stood
for that moral concern. He symbolizes among other things the human and social possibility of equality. This is the moral question
raised in our two great nineteenth-century novels, *Moby Dick* and
Huckleberry Finn. The very center of Twain's book revolves finally
around the boy's relations with Nigger Jim and the question of
what Huck should do about getting Jim free after the two scoun-
drels had sold him. There is a magic here worth conjuring, and
that reaches to the very nerve of the American consciousness—so

why should I abandon it? Our so-called race problem has now lined up with the world problems of colonialism and the struggle of the West to gain the allegiance of the remaining non-white people who have thus far remained outside the Communist sphere; thus its possibilities for art have increased rather than lessened. Looking at the novelist as manipulator and depictor of moral problems, I ask myself how much of the achievement of democratic ideals in the United States has been affected by the steady pressure of Negroes and those whites who were sensitive to the implications of our condition; and I know that without that pressure the position of our country before the world would be much more serious than it is even now. Here is part of the social dynamics of a great society. Perhaps the discomfort about protest in books by Negro authors comes because since the nineteenth century American literature has avoided profound moral searching. It was too painful, and besides, there were specific problems of language and form to which the writers could address themselves. They did wonderful things, but perhaps they left the real problems untouched. There are exceptions, of course, like Faulkner, who has been working the great moral theme all along, taking it up where Mark Twain put it down.

I feel that with my decision to devote myself to the novel I took on one of the responsibilities inherited by those who practice the craft in the United States: that of describing for all that fragment of the huge diverse American experience which I know best, and which offers me the possibility of contributing not only to the growth of the literature but to the shaping of the culture as I should like it to be. The American novel is in this sense a conquest of the frontier; as it describes our experience, it creates it.

4. Special Studies: Theme, Structure and Motif

Thomas A. Vogler

Invisible Man:
Somebodys Protest Novel

> This simply because I had a notion it somehow would be of help to
> that Kurtz whom at the time I did not see—you understand. He
> was just a word for me. I did not see the man in the name any more
> than you do. Do you see him? Do you see the story? Do you see
> anything?
>
> (Conrad)
>
> Oh say can you see . . . ?　　　　　　　　(National Anthem)

With Hemingway and Faulkner both dead, this is not a time
of recognized literary giants. The public, and critics too, are too
easily preoccupied with literary giantism, with finding the next
heir to the vacated throne. Publishers want their books to sell, and
are not very timid about making claims. Readers want to feel that
what they are reading is what they ought to be reading, in terms
that can only be reached from the vantage point of a historical
perspective. Our contemporary writers should, however, be looked
on and cherished as partly-realized potential, writers whose work
should not be idolized too much, nor ignored, but read with the
best awareness we can bring to them of their relationships to our
own lives and to the traditions they continue. Melville seemed to
be a distinctly minor writer to his own age. In 1945 all seventeen
of Faulkner's books were out of print. We should be chastened
and warned by examples like these, but not overly frightened in
our attempts to find something of value in our contemporary
writers.

With the belated advent of "Black Literature" it has become
even more difficult to find a long-term context in which to read
or discuss a novel like *Invisible Man*. Its relevance to the contemporary social problems of Black citizens can be used to reduce
it to the level of a documentary of the Black experience.[1] On the

---

Reprinted from the *Iowa Review*, I (Spring, 1970), 64–82, by permission of
the author and the *Iowa Review*. Copyright © 1970 by the *Iowa Review*.
[1] "To read such a book, for example, as Ralph Ellison's brilliant novel of 1952,
Invisible Man, is to find, among one's richest satisfactions, the sense of immersion in all the concrete materialities of Negro life. One hears the very
buzz and hum of Harlem in the racy, pungent speech of his West Indians and

other hand, its insistence on craft and analysis, its careful avoidance of the explicit advocation of action, can be passed off by the
activists as the "buggy jiving" of a white middle-class sellout, or
the ravings of a private ego trip. This latter trend is accurately
prophesied at the very end of the novel.[2] Most intolerable, perhaps,
is the approach taken by some critics of both colors, that the novel
is "pure" art, that a Negro writer has finally written his way into
the mainstream of some etherealized literary tradition.[3]

In spite of the present existence of what *Time* magazine calls,
in the jargon of the literary stockmarket, a "modest literary
boom," these are not good times for writers. There are as many
kinds of literary suicide available as there are writers, and the
hardest thing seems to be, not to write the first novel, but to
remain at the craft, writing for one's self and for the one imaginary
reader who will understand, rather than for the publisher, the
editor, the reviewer, the agent, the publicist, and the novelty-
seeking audience they serve. But it is not enough of a problem for
the writer to be in an arena where public relations men largely
determine whether his book will sell less than 5,000 or more than
100,000 copies. There is also the problem of the critics, who are
committed in their own way to thinking of the literary stockmarket. Critics quite easily become obsessed with what is for them
the counterpart to the writer's creative urge. This is the desire
to find patterns comprehensive enough to include everything that
is good, and it is a reasonable enough urge when followed with
discrimination. But too easily the pattern becomes a definition
of what is good, and good writers get lost or distorted because they

---

his native hipsters, and all the *grotesquerie* in his opening account of the
dreary little backwater of a remote Southern Negro college has in it a certain kind of empirically absolute rightness. Indeed, the book is packed full of
the acutest observations of the manners and idioms and human styles that
comprise the ethos of Negro life in the American metropolis; and it gives us
such a sense of social fact as can be come by nowhere in the stiffly pedantic
manuals of academic sociology." Nathan A. Scott, Jr., "The Dark and
Haunted Tower of Richard Wright," *Black Expression,* ed. Addison Gayle,
Jr. (N.Y., 1969), p. 298.

[2] Cf. Leroi Jones' "The Myth of a Negro Literature," where all Black writers
are committed to mediocrity because "The literary and artistic models were
always those that could be socially acceptable to the white middle class,
which automatically limited them to the most spiritually debilitated imita-
tions of literature available." (*Black Expression,* p. 192)

[3] Worth noting for its grotesque insistence on this point, while at the same
time contradicting it with a reputed social message ("Ellison's hero . . .
is one of those catastrophic individuals of which society must rid itself before
there can be peace and sanity.") is Nancy Tischler's "Negro Literature and
Classic Form," *Contemporary Literature,* X, No. 3 (Summer 1969).

do not fit the mold. The critic of contemporary writers is especially
vulnerable to this mistake. As Norman Mailer pointed out, it is
"naturally wiser for the mind of the expert to masticate the
themes of ten writers, rather than approach the difficulties of any
one."

In many ways, then, to talk about a contemporary novel like
Invisible Man involves problems different from those we face when
discussing a novelist like Wharton or Fitzgerald. On the other
hand, no really good writer can be completely contemporary without serious limitations. The kind of synthesis and evaluation of
experience that we expect in a good novel cannot be contemporary
with the experience itself. In addition, Ellison has roots in the
19th century that are at least as important as those in the 20th;
what he writes is as much influenced by what he has read as it is
by what he has seen and lived through. Though Ellison is close
to Hemingway in many ways, and even copied his stories by hand
in order to develop an understanding of his style, he seems to bear
an even more important relationship to Melville. Ellison uses two
quotations as epigraphs at the beginning of *Invisible Man.* One,
from Melville's *Benito Cereno*, suggests the nature of the change
the invisible man undergoes in the novel. The other, from Eliot,
suggests the discovery of his invisibility which is an essential part
of the change. Before discussing invisibility and change, however,
I would like to suggest another passage, also from Melville, which
will help to get at some of the more negative aspects of the book—
for Ellison, like Melville, understood that fiction must be negative
in order to fulfill both its artistic and moral obligations:

> There is the grand truth about Nathaniel Hawthorne. He says NO!
> in thunder; but the devil himself cannot make him say yes. For all
> men who say yes, *lie;* and all men who say no,—why they are in
> the happy condition of judicious, unincumbered travellers in Eu-
> rope; they cross the frontiers into Eternity with nothing but a car-
> petbag—that is to say, Ego.

There is a nice comparison here with the invisible man, who crosses
his frontier into the darkness with a briefcase containing all the
clues to his identity or "Ego"; but the passage also suggests the
dark impulse of resistance which continues to permeate contemporary fiction in works like *Invisible Man.* The novelists seem to
agree that violence and distortion must be the means of projecting
a vision to which society is hostile. They seem further to agree
that the contemporary world presents a continued affront to man,

and that his response must therefore be at least in part that of the rebel.

There is a standard psychological experiment known to produce neuroses and psychopathic behavior patterns in most domestic or trainable animals. In an experimental environment that bears a striking resemblance to the world of the novel, the animals are trained to react in certain ways to certain stimuli, and then placed in a situation in which the reactions are impossible. The animal then makes what attempts it can to go on acting as it has been trained to do, but with continued frustration a nervous collapse of some kind inevitably follows. With some, the reaction is solipsistic—they refuse to mix with other animals even for eating. Others react by batting their heads against the walls of their cages until they die or are too exhausted to continue. The equivalent experience of conflict between expectations and reality has produced what Ellison calls "the American Negro impulse toward self-annihilation and going underground," which can only be overcome by "a will to confront the world, to evaluate his experience honestly and throw his findings unashamedly into the guilty conscience of America." [4] His *Invisible Man* is a record of that agony, and of the discovery of the realities that must be faced before a genuine identity can be achieved.

> But I think the memoir, which is titled *Invisible Man,* his memoir, is an attempt to describe reality as it really exists rather than in terms of what he had assumed it to be. Because it was the clash between his assumptions, his illusions about reality, and its actual shape which made for his agony. [5]

In the novel we see the kind of training the invisible man is subjected to most clearly in the chapel scene in Chapter 5. Here are Barbee's concluding remarks, holding up Bledsoe as the pattern for the hero to follow:

> His is a form of greatness worthy of your imitation. I say to you, pattern yourselves upon him. Aspire, each of you, to someday follow in his footsteps.

In the next chapter, Bledsoe tries to explain to the invisible man what he calls "the difference between the way things are and the way they're supposed to be," but it is a lesson he is not yet pre-

---

[4] "Richard Wright's Blues" (*Black Expression,* p. 325).
[5] "An Interview with Ralph Ellison," *Tamarack Review,* No. 32 (Summer 1964), p. 11.

pared to learn. The invisible man, like most of us, is living in a culture whose incentives, rewards and punishments prevent the development of the kind of personal standards which the public ideals demand for a feeling of self-respect. He is in the situation Paul Goodman describes in *Growing up Absurd,* where the only truly healthy response is to reject those parts of society that threaten his own possibilities for self-respect. But he cannot reject them without knowing what they are, and they are built in so that he is himself responsible for much of what he must go through.

To call a novel a protest novel at this point of history is inevitably to call back the thirties and the great American discovery of social injustice. The roots of much in *Invisible Man* are to be found in this period, in writers like Dos Passos, Steinbeck, Farrell, Hemingway (at least in *For Whom the Bell Tolls*), and especially Richard Wright. During the forties there was a decline in novels dealing primarily with the social themes of the thirties; during this period, however, there was a constant discovery of new areas of social disorganization which novelists adopted for the focus of their works. The war experience was another catastrophe, piled on top of the depression, which the American novelist had to cope with in his attempts to find a view of his place in society. Another discovery during this period—and a much belated one—was of the extent and complexity of the social problems of the Negro, and of the essential part these problems took in any attempt to achieve an overall view of American society. The development of the Negro novel is not adequately explained by a theory of growing liberalism, or a shedding of prejudice which now makes white readers willing to read books they know were written by Blacks. It is not even clear that the early publishers, who disguised the fact that particular novels were written by Blacks, were acting realistically—but that's beside the point. What is clear is that in the 20th century, as in the 19th, the position of the Black citizen in our society is the *focus* of social and ideological polarities that go far beyond the question of race relations. It is also the focus for many of the neurotic fears and desires that are an inevitable part of our gross national product. From Richard Wright's first novel on, the movement has not been a shedding of prejudice, but a growing awareness, in writers and readers alike, of the essential centrality of the Black problem to any adequate view of American society.

Negro life is a byproduct of Western civilization, and in it, if only one possesses the humanity and humility to see, are to be discov-

ered all those impulses, tendencies, life and cultural forms to be
found elsewhere in Western society.[6]

It is in this way that Black writers have been developing and
expressing an awareness of the universal significance of their
position, as Faulkner had earlier found in a single southern county
all the elements necessary to an understanding of human nature
and the movement of history. Ellison is like Faulkner in seeing
the South as a land doomed by the curse of slavery, yet still with
a vestigial aura of Edenic simplicity. But Ellison follows his Black
hero out of the South, as Wright had done, and is much more
concerned than Faulkner with a direct consideration of the implications of the civil war, for all aspects of contemporary society,
both North and South.

It would be too simple a view to consider the function of the
Black protagonist as merely that of another outsider who can
serve as a foil to define weaknesses in the social structure. The
situation of the Black, like that of the writer, is a part of the
society and reveals important things about it.

> Anyway, in the beginning I thought that the white world was very
> different from the world I was moving out of and I turned out to be
> entirely wrong. It seemed different. It seemed safer, at least the
> white people seemed safer. It seemed clearer, it seemed more po-
> lite, and, of course, it seemed much richer from the material point
> of view. But I didn't meet anyone in that world who didn't suffer
> from the very same affliction that all the people I had fled from suf-
> fered from and that was that they didn't know who they were.
> They wanted to be something that they were not. And very shortly
> I didn't know who I was, either. I could not be certain whether I
> was really rich or really poor, really black or really white, really
> male or really female, really talented or a fraud, really strong or
> merely stubborn. In short, I had become an American.[7]

The final test of the mastery of illusion and reality, and the
discovery of an identity, is the ability to *tell* it. This is not the
novelist's prerogative, as the examples of Malcolm X and Eldridge
Cleaver show, and as Ellison suggests in Brother Tarp's recognition of the "signifying" embodied in his chain link and his pleasure
at finally being able to communicate his story to the invisible man

---

[6] *Black Expression*, p. 324.
[7] James Baldwin, "Notes for a Hypothetical Novel," *Nobody Knows My
Name* (N.Y., 1961), pp. 148–49.

("I'm tellin' it better'n I ever thought I could!"). If Ellison has entered the mainstream of modern art, it is through his fusion of the problems of his Black protagonist with those of the writer, whose search for form and reality is the central problem of most serious writers of fiction in the last 100 or so years. In an eloquent mood, Ellison has spoken to the best hopes of most novelists, of whatever color:

> Life is as the sea, art a ship in which man conquers life's crushing formlessness, reducing it to a course, a series of swells, tides and wind currents inscribed on a chart. Though drawn from the world, "the organized significance of art," writes Malraux, "is stronger than all the multiplicity of the world; ... that significance alone enables man to conquer chaos and to master destiny." [8]

Invisible Man is not 'just' a Negro novel then, and Ellison has been very careful throughout to avoid this tempting limitation, even while giving us a very comprehensive view of race relations in both the South and the North. Look for a moment at Tod Clifton, remembering that it is no accident that *Tod* in German means "death." Tod is part black, part white, symbolically gray like the "Liberty Paint" that goes out of the factory to decorate some important national monument. Tod's death is one of the key turning points of the book, forcing the invisible man to the recognition that we all shall die, leading finally to the recognition that, in an absurd society, it is an error to cater to any but one's own unique absurdity. His reflections on Tod's death are a turning-point from which he intensifies the exploration of his own identity and begins to recognize more fully the possible identities of others. In the crowd at the funeral oration he sees individual faces, marked with suffering that he begins to understand:

> Here are the facts. He was standing and he fell. He fell and he kneeled. He kneeled and he bled. He bled and he died. He fell in a heap like any man and his blood spilled out like any blood; red as any blood, wet as any blood—and it dried in the sun as blood dries. That's all.

The specific racial killing of a Black man becomes more than the death of an individual caused by social injustice. It is the death of the best parts of the individual caused by the worst parts of

---

[8] *Black Expression,* p. 316.

society; it is "OUR HOPE SHOT DOWN," for on the lower frequencies Ellison has been speaking for us all.

In *Invisible Man* we have a full portrait of the element of despair and of the destructive element forced on the Black, the writer, and on us as well if we go along. The question we are deliberately left with, in the end which is also a beginning, is the constructive use to which these elements can be put—the role for the self which has at last been recognized and accepted, the kind of life one can live in a realm of absurdity which is also a realm of possibility. The problem of how all this negation can be put to use is already answered in part by the very existence of the novel. It is emphasized in the beginning and end that the protagonist of the book is also its creator, and that the writing of the book is itself part of the experience, and of the discovery of an identity, which is the subject of the book. What is affirmative in both the structure and the existence of the book is that the invisible man does survive through turning his experience into art. In the same way, the ordinary Black in a hostile society has been able to turn daily injustice and suffering into the folk art of the blues. The novel, like the blues, offers a way of standing apart from one's experience without losing its intensity or its meaning. All Black writers have agreed that the blues have been a survival mechanism for the Negro in America and also that they have been the most important cultural contribution to American art. For Ellison, the blues "is an impulse to keep the painful details and episodes of a brutal experience alive in one's aching consciousness, to finger its jagged grain, and to transcend it, not by the consolation of philosophy, but by squeezing from it a near-tragic, near-comic lyricism." The blues recognizes both the painful and contradictory aspects of experience, turning them into something like a joke. "There is a mystery in the whiteness of blackness, the innocence of evil, and the evil of innocence, though, being initiates, Negroes express the joke of it in the blues." The acceptance is finally achieved only in terms of artistic expression, whether it be in the blues or in the form and creation of a novel. In the book itself, this analogy with the blues is continually suggested. In some cases, as in the college chapel scene, the blues can be an expression of hope:

> I closed my eyes as I heard the deep moaning sound that issued from him, and the rising crescendo of the student body joining in. This time it was music sincerely felt, not rendered for the guests, but for themselves; a song of hope and exaltation. I wanted to rush from the building, but didn't dare. I sat stiff and erect, supported by the hard bench, relying upon it as upon a form of hope.

In other cases, such as the singing at Tod Clifton's funeral, the invisible man comes closer to recognizing the sense of blues that Ellison was getting at in his definition. Here is his reaction to the man who starts the singing:

> I looked into the face of the old man who had aroused the song and felt a twinge of envy. It was a worn, old, yellow face and his eyes were closed and I could see a knife welt around his upturned neck as his throat threw out the song. . . . I watched him now, wet-eyed, and I felt a wonder at the singing mass. It was as though the song had been there all the time, and he knew it and aroused it; And I knew that I had known it too, and had failed to release it out of a vague, nameless shame or fear. Even white brothers and sisters were joining in. Something deep had shaken the crowd, and the old man and the man with the horn had done it. They had touched upon something deeper than protest or religion. It was not the words, for they were all the same old slave-borne words: it was as though he'd changed the emotion beneath the words while yet the old longing, resigned, transcendent emotion still sounded above, now deepened by that something for which the theory of brother-hood had given me no name.

The invisible man has found something here that the conscious quest for identity had failed to reveal. It is only after this discovery that he is able to make of his writing the same use that the singer makes of the blues. It is a means of achieving an acute sense of identity and self-recognition that society has been unable to provide.[9]

---

[9] In "The Discovery of What it Means to be an American" Baldwin describes what he calls "a species of breakdown," and how he was cured of it by listening to Bessie Smith on records. He wrote *Go Tell It on the Mountain* "armed with two Bessie Smith records and a typewriter," as the invisible man writes his story listening to Louis Armstrong. There is a passage in Part III of *Go Tell It on the Mountain* where John Grimes undergoes an experience comparable to the invisible man's, in almost the same words that I have quoted from Ellison:

> He had heard it all his life, but it was only now that his ears were opened to this sound that came from the darkness, that could only come from darkness, that yet bore such sure witness to the glory of the light. And now in his moaning, and so far from any help, he heard it in himself—it rose from his bleeding, his cracked-open heart. It was a sound of rage and weeping which filled the grave, rage and weeping from time set free, but bound now in eternity; rage that had no language, weeping with no voice—which yet spoke now, to John's startled soul, of boundless melancholy, of the bitterest patience, and the longest night; of the deepest water, the strongest chains, the most cruel lash; of humility most wretched, the dungeon most absolute, of love's bed defiled, and birth dishonored, and most bloody, unspeakable, sudden death. Yes, the darkness hummed with murder; the body in the water, the body in the fire, the

This discovery of the potential for self-discovery in the blues, or in a novel which approaches them in spirit, comes on the invisible man almost unawares, in spite of the more literary and more conscious quest for identity that he has been pursuing before. Sooner or later it seems that almost every modern work can in some way be read as a search—or more typically a "quest"—for a father or a mother. The two concepts are not interchangeable; they offer primitive but different solutions to man's basic need to reach beyond his own mind and find some fixed point around which to orient his own existence. The search for a father is almost always for a principle of authority, a lawgiver of some kind, even if it is the stern inscrutability of some abstract principle of necessity. In the earlier part of *Invisible Man* we find figures like the Founder and Bledsoe, and the great white father figures of Norton and the other trustees. Even the Brotherhood, at first felt as a fraternity of equality and freedom, is finally seen to be dominated by a harshly paternal theory of history, and Brother Jack turns out to be a disguised father masquerading as a brother. The mother figure typically offers an alternative orientation for experience, and has something that is always missing or of lesser importance in the father figures. The strictness of the father is replaced by the all-embracing acceptance of the mother, who refuses to reject her child no matter how poor, weak or sinful he has become. In *Invisible Man* the landlady Mary who takes up the hero and keeps him and feeds him is such a figure. He is trying to reach Mary's when he falls down the hole at the end, and it is to Mary's that his feet had unconsciously taken him earlier in the book:

> But I was never to reach Mary's. And now I realized that I couldn't return to Mary's, to any part of my old life, I could only approach it from the outside, and I had been as invisible to Mary as I had been to the brotherhood.

The recognition that he can't return to Mary, that the alternative she suggests, with all its religious overtones, is as unattainable as that offered by the series of fathers, is paralleled by the tone and structure Ellison uses to handle the theme in the novel. The invisible man's search for a father or a mother is a reflex in him, and therefore an inevitable part of his experience and a necessary part of the novel. But if the novel must go through the quest because

---

body on the tree. John looked down the line of these armies of darkness, army upon army, and his soul whispered, *Who are these?* (p. 228)

its protagonist must go through, it can at least do it in a different way. Ellison has pointed out that "When you are influenced by a body of literature or art from an earlier period, it is usually the form of it that is available to you," and he has openly acknowledged the high degree of literary self-consciousness manifest in the novel. "Let's put it this way—I'm a highly conscious writer. I know what's been done because I've read the books, I've studied them." [10] The consciousness of form and archetype leads to a deliberate and parodic use of such patterns in Ellison's work, and contributes to its enlightened literary humor. The invisible man may be duped into questing after unattainable or irrelevant goals, but he will not let his novel make the same mistake. The more innovative quest in *Invisible Man* is not that for a father or a mother, but the search for a group, a fraternity, a brotherhood of fellow humans in which the invisible man can find his identity and achieve the freedom and dignity which are the real goals of his quest. The final irony of this quest is that the real brotherhood, that of all humans facing death and oppression, can be joined only by renouncing all fictitious bases of brotherhood. In every alternative but this, the invisible man must repress part of his emotions and his humanity—the group of Black boys in the battle-royal, his fellow students, the union, the catch-all fraternity of the Harlem Men's House, the disguised paternal system of the Brotherhood, the Black fraternity of Ras the Exhorter-Destroyer—all of these offer roles which he either cannot accept or which demand that he sacrifice too much of himself to find a genuine identity in membership.

As he moves from one tentative role to another, he attempts to cast off earlier parts of his identity which the new roles cannot accept. Simultaneously with becoming a brother, he trys to discard the bank which is an image of different kinds of dependencies. "Feed me," the bank says on its front, and it reminds us of all the Black entertainers who have publicly distorted themselves into this gross caricature, just as the invisible man's attempts to destroy the bank suggest the corps of jazz musicians who have refused to smile while playing in order to prevent associations with the old image from coming back to destroy the dignity of their art. In spite of his attempts, the invisible man cannot get rid of the bank. A white woman, and a white man, force him to retrieve it first out of the garbage and then off the street. So he seals it up

---

[10] *Tamarack Review,* pp. 5–6.

in the briefcase with all the other clues to the identity which he refuses to accept. The briefcase is an emblem of himself, a container of images which he hates but cannot lose:

> "What's in that briefcase," they said, and if they'd asked me anything else I might have stood still. But at the question a wave of shame and outrage shook me and I ran.

This is the same question the doctors were asking him earlier, only now he is ready to find the answer. He is forced, in the darkness of his hole, to explore the contents of the briefcase which are the real clues to his identity and the only source of light.

The exploration, as I have already suggested, is undertaken in the act of telling the story. In this exploration the big issues are the problems of politics, of freedom, of brotherhood, of the rejection of a father and the loss of a mother, the distrust of rhetoric and abstractions which dilute experience and disguise reality. All of these issues are elements in the formal pattern and structure of the novel. But all of these are tied together by the central problem of finding his identity. Until he finds it, the invisible man is like a cup of water without the cup; he takes on his identity from whatever shape his environment offers until, finally, he realizes that his once new and clean briefcase, now battered and dirty, is symbolically the container of all the clues that are essential to finding his true identity. This chameleon-like flexibility is one of the most typically American features in the whole book, and it is perhaps our best clue to Ellison's identity as an American writer. From the legendary versatility of Benjamin Franklin, through innumerable characters in Irving, Hawthorne, Melville, Whitman and Twain, there is the concept of a character who can move from one identity to another without effort, preparation or reflection. This concept is so basic that it turns up both in the traditions and idealized national myths—characters like Franklin and Alger—and in the works of writers like Ellison who are rebelling from the hypocrisy of those ideals while still realizing that metamorphosis is a basic fact and possibility of existence. It can be a debased, almost subhuman instrument of survival, as in Faulkner's Snopse family, or it can be a social triumph as in the legendary founder of the invisible man's college. It can be the source of humor, as in *Huckleberry Finn*, or the more cosmic and ironic humor of Melville's *Confidence Man*.[11]

---

[11] It can also be the subject of a book, as in Sister Bernetta Quinn's *Metamorphic Tradition in Modern Poetry*, and Daniel Hoffman's *Form and Fable in American Fiction*.

At a crucial point in the novel the invisible man "discovers" this principle of metamorphosis which has been there all along. At first, he is impressed by the world of possibilities opened up before him:

> Well, I *was* and yet I was invisible, that was the fundamental contradiction. I was and yet I was unseen. It was frightening and as I sat there I sensed another frightening world of possibilities.... Perhaps I could tell them to hope until I found the basis of something real, some firm ground for action.... But until then I would have to move them without myself being moved ... I'd have to do a Rinehart.

So he tries to Rinehart it; he will find a woman in the Brotherhood and use her to gain inside information about their plans. Unfortunately for the invisible man he picks Sybil for his informant, and she has the enthusiastic frenzy but lacks the information he is looking for.[12] Instead, she merely gives him another lesson in his invisibility. She looks through him and sees nothing but her own fantasy of the Black phallus, the Negro rapist. And since he is now "doing a Rinehart" as he puts it, operating in the world of possibility, he can convince her—or let her convince herself—that she was raped without actually doing it. "SYBIL, YOU WERE RAPED BY SANTA CLAUS SURPRISE" he writes on her bare belly. And the image is a perfect one, for her fantasy of him is no more real than the child's fantasy. She has been taught to believe in the Black sex fantasy as the child is taught to believe in the great magic gift-giver.[13]

There is an interesting example of the precision and economy of Ellison's characterization in this episode. There are two sexual adventures in the book, and they both serve distinct functions. The first adventure occurred when the invisible man was sent downtown to lecture on "The Woman Question," only to find out that the real question was the one Ras had asked earlier, when trying to understand what could move a Black to join the Brotherhood. What is it, Ras asks, money or women, that is confusing the invisible man's ideology. The woman who seduces him in her apartment is confusing the concept of brotherhood with biology, offering

---

[12] In classical times sibyls or *sibyllae* were young maidens dwelling in lonely caves or by inspiring springs. Their function was to give forth prophetic utterances while under the influence of an enthusiastic frenzy.

[13] Mailer's essay "The White Negro" is a more sophisticated or Hip version of this same fantasy. Baldwin, in "The Black Boy Looks at the White Boy," acknowledges that "to be an American Negro male is also to be a kind of walking phallic symbol: which means that one pays, in one's own personality, for the sexual insecurity of others."

in fact still another alternative that he must try and then reject during the novel.

> Why did they have to mix their women into everything? Between us and everything we wanted to change in the world they placed a woman: socially, politically, economically. Why, godammit, why did they insist upon confusing the class struggle with the ass struggle, debasing both us and them—all human motives.

This is the other side of the confusion that Ras showed on the woman question. They both attribute a sexual motivation to a drive to attain social equality and human dignity.

The principle of invisibility and projected fantasy which we have seen operating in these episodes—and which the invisible man is gradually discovering was announced on the first page of the novel. It is "a peculiar disposition of the eyes of those with whom I come in contact. A matter of the construction of their *inner* eyes, those eyes with which they look through their physical eyes upon reality." The consequence of this disposition of the inner eye for the invisible man is not that people see nothing at all when they look in his direction, for they know that *something* is there. What they do is look through that something at what they expect to see, what they think is there—the inner eye sees a fiction that it has itself created. The first concrete example of this error of vision comes in the Prologue, when the invisible man bumps into a tall blond man who insults him and curses him when asked to apologize. In the fight that follows the white man is almost killed, but not by the invisible man. "Something in this man's thick head had sprung out and beaten him within an inch of his life," and that something was the man's own prejudiced concept of the Nigger which he had insulted and cursed.

The Prologue also introduces the problem of names which the reader encounters with almost every character, and the critic suffers while trying to write about the nameless protagonist of the novel. Thoreau once wrote an essay largely devoted to praising the system of naming practiced by the American Indians. What Thoreau admired about the system was the idea that everyone had to wait until he had earned a name through some significant action, or until he had revealed enough of his basic personality for a name to be chosen that adequately reflected his individuality. The "invisible man" is an earned name in something like the same sense, as "Jack the Bear" is his underground name because he sees his underground time as a period of hibernation. Most of the names we are given for characters in the novel are also earned names, or names which serve as clues to the character's nature or his function in the novel. Sometimes these names are symbolic, like "Tod" Clifton or "Mary." More often they are not so much directly symbolic as suggestive.

For example, when we look at Brother Jack, we should remember that a common slang meaning for "jack" is money. The name emphasizes the financial element in the relationship between the invisible man and the Brotherhood. When Ras ("race") the Exhorter asked whether it was money or women that could blind a Negro to his racial identity, the invisible man was outraged that his purity of motive could be questioned. But the whole scene takes place in front of a garish sign that says "CHECKS CASHED HERE." Brother Jack first showed up when the invisible man was out of money, and his first reason for joining the Brotherhood was for the pay they offered. Without knowing it, at the same time as he is trying to get rid of the bank because it is the image of the paid entertainer debasing himself for money, he is taking on an analogous position within the Brotherhood. This is emphasized at the end, when Brother Jack is disciplining him. ". . . you were not hired to think. Had you forgotten that? If so, listen to me: You were not hired to think."

Rinehart is another significant name, but it can be misleading if one looks to the German *rein* ("pure") for help. "Rind" (or "rine" in the pronunciation of the novel) is a good American slang word. If a person has a lot of rind, it means he has a lot of nerve. If he *is* a rind, it means he is thick-skinned in a sense ranging all the way from not caring what other people think to not caring what happens to them. This is the rind in the Rinehart in the novel, and the invisible man points to it just before hunting up Sybil:

> Now I recognized my invisibility. So I'd accept it, I'd explore it, rine and heart. I'd plunge into it with both feet and they'd gag. Oh, but wouldn't they gag.

As it turns out, however, it is the invisible man who gags on the rind, for he is not cynical enough to keep up the role. "Such games were for Rinehart, not me," he says, and he washes off the lipstick inscription he had meant to leave behind. Meanwhile, by doing a Rinehart, by pretending to agree with the Brotherhood in order to undermine it, he does in effect agree, and becomes a betrayer of the Harlem Brothers while working in his own interests. The irony of this role is that in the very moment of seeing Sybil's fantasy of the Black rapist he is himself attempting to live one. Rinehart, the "spiritual technologist" is like the nameless Black Doctor in Barth's *End of the Road,* offering a "Mythotherapy" for role-paralysis which works only until one must face the consequences of his arbitrary action.

"Emerson" is another important name in *Invisible Man,* and one Ellison is acutely aware of as that of his own namesake. He deliberately uses it to undercut the conventional liberal attitude towards race relations, when the *son* of old Emerson (to suggest the historical continuity) tries to befriend the invisible man. Young Emerson tries to find him a place in the great Liberty Paint company just as Norton had tried to help him find a place in the American society, but both Norton and Emerson have an image of *the* Negro which limits their possibility of sharing any kind of reality with the invisible man. Emerson even wants to find a place for him in his own confused private life; after announcing that he had "a difficult session" with his analyst the evening before, Emerson goes on:

> "Some things are just too unjust for words," he said, expelling a plume of smoke, "and too ambiguous for either speech or ideas. By the way, have you ever been to the Club Calamus?"
> "I don't think I've ever heard of it, sir," I said.
> "You haven't? It's very well known. Many of my Harlem friends go there. It's a rendezvous for writers, artists and all kinds of celebrities. There's nothing like it in the city, and by some strange twist it has a truly continental flavor."

The fey tone of this speech alone is enough to destroy what little respect we might have had for Emerson, but the Calamus Club reference takes it a bit further. The allusion is to the group of Whitman poems commonly called the Calamus Poems and dealing in a subtle but unmistakeable way with the theme of homosexuality. In other words, here is still another fraternity or Brotherhood that is being offered the invisible man, and as the historical Emerson's ideas are debased in his 20th-century "son," Whitman's androgynously cosmic appetite is reduced to a stylish sexual mystique. Emerson makes it even more explicit later, when he says "... I'm Huckleberry, you see. ..." in hopes that the invisible man will be another Jim, and perhaps have read Leslie Fiedler. But the invisible man can't be Jim because he is already too busy being Huckleberry himself without knowing it.

Characters' names, and the club names, and the names of factories, places and institutions—even the names of things, like the Sambo doll—can be explored indefinitely in this novel. The Brotherhood has its parties at a place called the Chthonian Club, which is a classical reference comparable to that of the Sybils. The Chthonian realm belonged to the underground gods and spirits; and true power for Ellison is an underground influence as we learn from seeing Bledsoe and Brockway and Brother Jack in action, as well as the invisible man writing in his hole. Where does Ras get his name, with its vocal nearness to "race?" He gives it to himself, as the invisible man gives us the name we must call him by if we are to know him for what he is.

The invisible man in action is an image collector or symbolist, gathering up into his briefcase all the concrete emblems and reminders of his experience that can serve as clues to finding his real name and identity. The book itself is for the reader a similar container of images and clues expanded into actions and events. The first example of an action-as-image after the Prologue is the battle royal scene which opens the story. If we explored this scene far enough, we could find in it a prefiguration of almost everything else in the novel. Before the battle, the boys are forced to look at the naked blond dancing for the whites. In the battle we see a group of half-naked Black boys, blindfolded, fighting each other in a ring for the entertainment of a group of white citizens. Afterwards, they fight again, still among themselves, for the coins on the electrified rug. The coins they desire the most, the gold ones, turn out to be brass, but there are enough dollars to go around. Afterwards, the invisible man steps forward and gives his carefully-prepared speech (with one prophetic verbal slip) in which he defends the status quo of the Southern Negro who is trying to better himself through education in segregated schools. These are the bare bones of the scene, and they are suggestive in themselves. But if we look closer we can see much more. The naked white girl with golden hair suggests and prefigures the whole problem of money and sex. Her golden hair, like the fake golden coins, holds out a promise of a world which can never exist for the invisible man because it too is brass. The blindfolds on the boys are white blindfolds, and the darkness they are fighting in is a darkness imposed upon them by the white spectators who represent the whole society:

They were all there—bankers, lawyers, judges, doctors, fire chiefs, teachers, merchants. Even one of the more fashionable pastors.

They unleash a great deal of violence in their brawl, but it is all directed against themselves, under the control of and for the amusement of this representative audience. During the brawl one of the boys, the invisible man, loosens his blindfold enough so that he can make out a little bit of what is going on. And it is this one who comes forward afterwards to speak to the crowd, as the invisible man is speaking to us in the novel.

In the first few pages of the book, this scene seems to be primarily a description of what happened to a few people at a particular "smoker" in some small unidentified southern town. But as we read through the book, with this scene planted in our memories, we gradually realize that in it is condensed the whole world of the novel and almost all of the American society. The final scene, the race riot in Harlom, is in large part a repetition of the beginning scene, but one which we can more easily relate to the larger context it represents. Instead of the coins on the electrified rug, there is the safe on the third rail showering the streets with sparks. Instead of control being in ordinary citizens, it is in Brother Jack who represents their interests in controlling the Blacks. Instead of Tatlock and the invisible man battling it out at the end for supremacy, we have Ras and the invisible man, finally silencing his fanatic appeal to race by throwing a spear through his jaws. The riot is probably the most impressively sustained section of the whole novel. It is still carefully kept to the elements already prefigured in the brawl, yet expanded into a comic apocalypse of enormous proportions. It begins as a drunken orgy of consumer wish-fulfillment which is a fantasy Christmas ("At St. Nicholas the street lights were out.") and fourth of July combined. At the peak of their frenzied rebellion the looters are still being controlled and manipulated by society's official symbol-makers:

> "With all them hats in there and I'm going to come out with anything but a *Dobbs?* Man, are you *mad?* All them new, pretty-colored *Dobbs?*"

> "Git a side of bacon, Joe," a woman called. "Git a side of bacon, Joe, git Wilson's."

Even Ras, who now calls himself the "Destroyer," has made himself up from the scrap heap of cultural detritus as Quixote made himself up from scraps and pieces of the old Romances. He is a composite of cowboy and African movies, equipped with stage-prop lion skin, spear and shield, "one of the kind you see them African guys carrying in the moving pictures...." Although they are rioting against society, no one knows how the riot got started, and the only damage they succeed doing is to themselves in the pathetic burning-down of their own tenement. The only difference, save that of scale, is that at the end the invisible man does not step forward and give a speech prepared for him by the cultural myths, but instead disappears down his hole and creates a book which could only be written after he had recognized his invisibility.

On a smaller scale we can see the same kind of significance at work throughout the novel. In fact, there is a whole scale of images at work at almost every point in *Invisible Man*. Small ones, like the statue of the Founder removing the veil from the slave, but seen in such a way that it is impossible to tell whether it is being removed or put more firmly in place—echoed later by the invisible man's spotlight blindness as he makes his first official Brotherhood speech. Another is the recurring image of the mounted police, controlling the animal power of their black horses through a more efficient power and technique. In the invisible man's Brotherhood office is a map of the world with the figure of Columbus, reminding us that the real America is yet to be discovered, and that although there may be natives there, they will not be the natives we expected to find.

Some of these images seem to be quite clearly intended for the reader alone. Although they are registered through the eyes and consciousness of the invisible man, they are not noted by him as containing any special significance. In the El Toro bar, there are two bullfight posters which are described matter-of-factly along with the other miscellaneous contents of the room. The first poster shows a large black bull, being skillfully controlled by the matador. The other poster shows the tables turned, the bull finally discovering the illusion of the cape and tossing the matador high into the air. This is much like the fight between a prizefighter and a yokel described in the Prologue, where "the yokel, rolling about in the gale of boxing gloves, struck one blow and knocked science, speed and footwork as cold as a well-digger's posterior. The smart money hit the canvas. The long shot got the nod." The bullfight posters, and their echo of the prizefight, are a silent comment on the discussion going on in the bar between Brother Jack—who is trying to discipline him—and the invisible man. They are also a prediction of the outcome of the contest which will be fulfilled later in the novel.

Another condensed prefiguration is carefully suggested in the scene where Brother Tarp gives the invisible man his severed chain link, telling him the story of his limp which the doctors can't explain. For "saying no" to a man who wanted to take something from him, Tarp lost his wife, children and land and was sentenced to a life in prison on a chain gang. Nineteen years later, he said no again, and kept saying it until he broke the chain and left. Still limping, and still "looking for freedom," he gives the link to the invisible man because "it's got a heap of signifying wrapped up in it and it might help you to remember what we're really fighting against." At the moment of giving him the link, Tarp stops calling him son and calls him Brother "for the first time." The ceremony is

> like a man passing on to his son his own father's watch, which the son accepted not because he wanted the old-fashioned time-piece for itself, but because of the overtones of unstated seriousness and solemnity of the paternal gesture which at once joined him with his ancestors, marked a high point of his present, and promised a concreteness to his nebulous and chaotic future. And now I remembered that if I had returned home instead of coming north my father would have given me my grandfather's old-fashioned Hamilton, with its long, burr-headed winding stem.

Tarp is both his spiritual father and brother, for they are looking for freedom together by saying no to slavery which has left its mark on each of them. Had the invisible man stayed in the South, in his own father's and grandfather's tradition, he would have remained a "burr-head" and a slave without knowing it.

Although some of these images are like guideposts for the reader, reminding him of the larger pattern of the novel, the larger ones are all in some degree meaningful to the invisible man, and there is a consistent pattern in his reaction to them. After each significant event, he gives a speech which summarizes his state of development as of that moment in the novel. The most naive speech is the one he gives after the brawl. In each succeeding recognition he is at least potentially more aware of who he is and what his experience means until the point where he is able to summarize the whole in a book which *includes* the other speeches. An example of the tentative progression of these speeches can be seen in Chapter 13. After having had his old identity wiped out through the boiler explosion, he begins to find a feeling of his own identity in a self-conscious but unashamed acceptance of some of the shabbier aspects of Harlem life. He eats a yam on the streets, without fear of being seen. When he comes on the eviction, he is at first embarrassed by the naked exposure of all the odds and ends of junk that tell the story of the life this old couple has lived. But gradually, as the furniture and debris pile up, he begins to realize that the belongings of the couple tell the story of his race, going all the way back to the Free Papers dated August, 1859. Even the consciousness of shame instilled in him from the day he was born can't obliterate the feeling of identity he gets from seeing these things:

> And it was as though I myself was being dispossessed of some painful yet precious thing which I could not bear to lose; something confounding, like a rotted tooth that one would rather suffer indefinitely than endure the short, violent eruption of pain that would mark its removal. And with this sense of dispossession came a pang of vague recognition.

The recognition is vague but intense, and the intensity shows up in the speech he makes and his willingness to fight for a feeling he still cannot define or fully accept.

Most of the actions and images I have been discussing have a plausible existence in the real world, and the important thing is the sensitivity of vision we bring to them. No matter how subtly calculated we can afterwards see the effect to be, there is always the impression of a real event while we are reading. There are places in *Invisible Man*, however, where the action seems decidedly secondary to the ideas Ellison is trying to convey, where the priority of the ideas dominates so that we can't read without the attempt to translate the action back into the ideas. In these cases Ellison seems to share Ishmael's attitude towards what he calls "hideous and intolerable allegory," not believing in it at all, yet unable to resist the comic indulgence of his appetite for it.

The clearest example here is in the factory hospital scene, where the doctors try to remake the invisible man into the mechanical man he had been before, the subservient southern Negro who died when he attacked Brockway in the boiler room. When he wakes in the hospital his mind is a blank, and he only gradually becomes aware that the doctors are trying to achieve a machine-induced prefrontal lobotomy that will return him to his previous state. The whole scene is presented as a return to childhood followed by rebirth, including the cutting of the umbilical cord (the electric cord attached to the stomach node), followed by an alcohol rubdown by an efficient nurse. "You're a new man," the doctors pointedly tell him. On the way home from the hospital the "new man" is metamorphosed into *the* new man, the Biblical Adam, who even predicts his own fall. "And I felt that I would fall, *had* fallen," he says, and then looks across the aisle of the subway car to see "a young platinum blonde nibbling at a red Delicious apple." [14]

The same serio-comic intent is behind the 1,369 light bulbs that are made so much of in the Prologue. The light bulbs are his means of fighting the Monopolated Light and Power Company, and Ellison's way of illustrating the effects of a self-recognition on the power struggle that occupies most of the novel. After first finding his own light by burning the papers in the briefcase, he can begin to take revenge on the power monopoly that he has suffered under for so long. He is finally out of their control. He can't overthrow them, but he can undermine and weaken them by draining off part of their power. No writer would go to this extent for the sake of an idea alone, and there is a very pointed humor in much of Ellison's "allegory." The ironic, joking tone of the blues is continually showing through, as well as the pleasure Ellison obviously gets from the virtuoso manipulation of words. For a final example, consider the description of eating dessert in the hole. The invisible man is sitting there. He's blue, he's wondering why he's blue, and thinking what it means to be blue. And he's listening to Louis Armstrong playing and singing, "What Did I Do to Be so Black and Blue." He has just made a big point of being in the great American tradition, and now he is describing his favorite dessert of sloe gin and ice cream. As we visualize him pouring the red liquid over the white mound, we suddenly get the point of the color scheme he has been building up to emphasize his Americanism, and the submerged but deliberate joke helps to establish the tone of the whole Prologue. The effect is almost gratuitously clever, but Ellison is a fierce punster, and he can't always restrict himself to the obvious level of "I yam what I am," or turning Brother Tobitts into two bits.

He is also a prophetic writer, and that is why I must conclude with the envelope or frame which makes up the novel's beginning and end. The Prologue gives us a picture of the invisible man after he's finished writing the book, a picture of his present state.

---

[14] This scene is reminiscent of Hart Crane's "For the Marriage of Faustus and Helen," where the poet-Faust imagines meeting Helen in a New York subway:

> And yet, suppose some evening I forgot
> The fare and transfer, yet got by that way
> Without recall—lost yet poised in traffic.
> Then I might find your eyes across an aisle,
> Still flickering with those prefigurations—
> Prodigal, yet uncontested now,
> Half-riant before the jerky window frame.

He has discovered that he is invisible, and taken the first step that he must take after the discovery. He has preserved his anger and his suffering by embodying it in art, and has even more fully grasped his identity in the process. But what is he to do with his identity after this, and after all the emphasis in the Epilogue on "the possibility that even an invisible man has a socially responsible role to play." We know that he is in hibernation, and we can't help wondering with him whether he will come up to find the smell of death or the smell of spring in the outside air. The invisible man doesn't know; he is prepared for a rebirth, and a new life, but has not yet been born into it. About 35 years ago Henry Roth published *Call it Sleep*. It was an extremely good novel, and for a first novel almost unbelievably good. Those were depression times, and it wasn't a protest novel, so there was not a great reaction, but those few who did appreciate it looked forward with anticipation to Roth's next work. While they waited, however, Roth disappeared, and has only recently been discovered, raising game birds near Augusta, Maine. With the rediscovery and tardy acclaim of *Call it Sleep*, many readers have naturally wondered why Roth has not written anything for so long. It turns out that he has been trying to write off and on, but can't. His problem, he says, is that "There is one theme I like above all others, and that is redemption, but I haven't the fable."

Invisible Man is clearly a prelude to and preparation for something like redemption, and therefore an extremely dangerous and difficult novel to follow. It may be that Ellison has written himself into a corner, or it may be that in his next novel he will find the fable for us. It seems to me that, if any of our contemporary writers can find it and express it, he can. But it has to be there first to be found, and whether it exists or not cannot be answered until it *is* found. Ellison has been working on his second novel for a long time now. Whatever he is doing, there is some evidence that it will be apocalyptic, that it will attempt to show us either the pattern of our redemption or of our destruction and continued frustration. We shouldn't forget that the alternative to a vision of redemption is carefully planted in the Prologue of *Invisible Man*. In his reflection on the brawl with the white man, the invisible man says:

He, let us say, was lost in a dream world. But didn't *he* control that dream world—which, alas, is only too real!—and didn't *he* rule me out of it? And if he had yelled for a policeman, wouldn't *I* have been taken for the offending one? Yes, yes, yes! Let me agree with

you, I was the irresponsible one; for I should have used my knife to
protect the higher interests of society. Some day that kind of fool-
ishness will cause us tragic trouble. All dreamers and sleepwalkers
must pay the price, and even the invisible victim is responsible for
the fate of all. But I shirked that responsibility; I became too snarled
in the incompatible notions that buzzed within my brain. I was a
coward. . . .

Marcus Klein

Ralph Ellison's "Invisible Man"

Ralph Ellison's invisible man speaks first of all for himself, a
Negro whose career, because he is a Negro, has been a search for
a primary, existential sense of himself. The existential question, as
a critic says, "lies waiting around the corner for any introspective
person, but it straddles the main highway for a thoughtful Negro." [1]
And despite the statement of faith with which *Invisible Man* ends,
that the hero can accomplish visibility, this invisible man speaks
in the conviction of utter failure.

In fact, the only way in which he might exist is in an enormous
act of vengeance, a mechanics which Bigger Thomas had discovered
before him. But the world is nothing so simple for him as it was for
Bigger. Simple murder won't do, and anyway he sees the contradic-
tion in vengeance. He accomplishes revenge and existence only at
a remove, in a nightmare underground. He is removed into nightmare not because it may be that in the ordinary ways of being, men
are inevitably determined, nor because there may be no such thing
as the existential self, nor because the gratuitous act may be really
gratuitous and without sense except in dreams. That would be certainly to open the universal theme. And he is condemned not

Reprinted from *After Alienation: American Novels in Mid-Century* (New
York: The World Publishing Company, 1964), pp. 249–64, by permission of
the publisher and the author. Copyright © 1964 by Marcus Klein.
[1] F. Cudworth Flint, "Fiction Chronicle," *Sewanee Review,* LXII (Winter,
1954), 176.

because of cowardice or lack of maturity—despite the fact Ellison has once commented on his hero's "refusal to run the risk of his own humanity, which involves guilt." [2] He is not a coward and he is very little guilty. And he is thrust into a nightmare not, despite the fact that Ellison has said it, because the frustration of identity is peculiarly the American theme. He is condemned first of all because he is black. The novel is glued to the fact. . . .

Out of the world and apart from ordinary defined experience is just where, in fact, the hero of the novel always finds himself. The large action of *Invisible Man* is all a circular voyage, consisting of four prominent adventures. It begins with a ritual of the hero's initiation, a test of his bravery, of his knowledge of caste, and of his sexuality, and it ends in failure, with the hero castrated, presented with proofs of his cowardice and ignorance, in a condition prior to his initiation. He is at the end back in the underworld from which he had tried to emerge, with this difference only, that he has illuminated his underworld and he now knows where he is.

That is the great irony the novel deliberately plays on itself— the world moves, the hero tells us in almost the first words of the Prologue, not like an arrow, nor in a spiral, but like a boomerang; his end, he says, is in his beginning. And it should be said immediately, the novel's great fault is in the fact that its end *is* its beginning. The novel is a furious picaresque which plunges the hero forward through a series of violences. Moreover, it is *all* an initiation rite. The hero moves from childhood to the age of manhood, and from the South to the North, and he is one of those heroes who move from the provinces to the capital, to the center of power, from innocence to experience. He moves, moreover, through what seems at all points a linear exploration of the "Negro problem," through ideologies by which it might be approached, and beyond that, through what one of the symbolic structures of the novel suggests is an exploration of some one hundred years of American history. But for all that multiplicity of parallel actions, the novel has no real progress except that at each stage it clarifies and reinforces the hero's dilemma.

---

[2] Ralph Ellison in an interview by Alfred Chester and Vilma Howard in *Paris Review*, No. 8 (Spring, 1955), 68. See also Ellison's statement to Rochelle Girson ("Sidelights on Invisibility," *Saturday Review*, XXXVI [March 14, 1953], 49): "Invisibility has to do with the failure of most of us to regard the individual we contact as a human being. . . . On the other hand, you have the failure of the individual to exert himself to be mature, to run the risk of humanity. . . ."

" 'Ah,' I can hear you say," the hero says in almost the last words of the Epilogue,

> "so it was all a build-up to bore us with his buggy jiving. He only wanted us to listen to him rave!" But only partially true: Being invisible and without substance, a disembodied voice, as it were, what else could I do? What else but try to tell you what was really happening when your eyes were looking through?

But the witness is not here being responsive to the witness against him. This appeal is a last-ditch attempt to rescue the book from what must have seemed to Ellison its strategic error. The amount of clarity the novel finally comes to is enormous, and so much clarity is shocking, but still it is a clarity without any further effect. The novel doesn't finally go anywhere.

It is a fault that apparently led Ellison to the desperate, empty, unreasonable, and programmatic optimism of the last few pages of the novel: "... we [Negroes] were to affirm the principle on which the country was built...." We "were linked to all others in the loud, clamoring semi-visible world...." "... I've overstayed my hibernation, since there's a possibility that even an invisible man has a socially responsible role to play." One asks this hero how he is to come out and be socially responsible? Upon what ground in reality can he affirm *any* positive principle? Just what is he going to do? Everything in the novel has clarified this point: that the bizarre accident that has led him to take up residence in an abandoned coal cellar is no accident at all, that the underworld is his inevitable home, that given the social facts of America, both invisibility and what he now calls his "hibernation" are his permanent condition. And really his only extension into the upper world can be in negative acts and fantasies of vengeance—which do indeed make up another ending to the novel.

And it is just another consequence of its circularity that *Invisible Man* has many endings. The novel sets out to gain clarity but no new discovery. Its ending is in its beginning. Therefore, with every gain in illumination, the novel concludes. There is a constant increase of wattage, but what is to be seen remains the same. And then the consequence of that fact is that—except in the Prologue and the Epilogue to the novel, where the hero speaks in time present and out of all his experience—the hero is fitted with a perceptiveness that is far inferior to Ellison's. Or, if not always, that becomes a fault. He is sometimes an *ingénu*, sometimes a naive

Gulliver when gullibility should be impossible, sometimes, suddenly, the author. There is a constant struggle between the two, Ellison straining not to let his protagonist know too much because that will give the book away, and sometimes failing. And finally the consequence of this latter fact is that a great deal of the novel is in a great density of symbols and puns. They don't, as the danger is, clog the action. They do contain the material. But they don't always contribute to the material. Because the hero can't know too much, because every discovery risks being the last discovery, because Ellison knows very well what each of his hero's experiences comes to, much of the hero's experience is converted into tantalizing hieroglyphics. The puns, which should be devices of compression, mount on each other and, like the major episodes of the novel, they tend each of them to tell the same and the whole story.

But then if at the end Ellison cops a plea—"what else could I do? What else but try to tell you what was really happening when your eyes were looking through?"—his plea is in every way valid. The novel's task is just the perception of obvious, repeated facts which no one sees. The task itself must be constantly emphasized and repeated in a great variety of ironic symbols, because that is a dramatic necessity in the nature of the task. The repetition is the proof that the task is authentic. The hero is first a high-school boy in a Southern town, then a college student at a Negro university, then, briefly, a laborer in a Northern factory, then a leader in what in the novel is called the Brotherhood, and finally an underground man. That is his whole story, all of it devoted to one struggle which is perpetual and obsessive because all his experience does really come to the same thing, an unremitting and fruitless attempt to achieve visibility. The book is filled by a lifetime of events, all of them leading back to the same meaning.

So in the Prologue, speaking of his invisibility in his coal cellar, the hero says he needs light because without it he is not only invisible but formless, and it is part of the joke he intends that he is, what someone calls him later, a nigger in a coal pile, that black can't be seen in the dark. The obvious is not obvious. The need is for illumination. And a series of leaders with whom the hero becomes engaged and who promise perception turn out to be blind. A Negro minister at his college, the Reverend Homer (Blind Homer) A. Barbee, preaches a sermon of hope, faith, and endurance, and falls flat on his face. Brother Jack, the local leader of the Brotherhood, sees salvation in the dialectic of historical necessity and can't see a thing because he has a glass eye, just because he has given his eye to the Brotherhood's vision. The Founder of the hero's Negro college, a great leader of his people and a thin disguise for the hero's first hero, Booker T. Washington, is presented to him first in an ambiguous statue in which the Founder is either lifting a veil from the face of a slave or lowering it.

And the task the novel sets for itself, perception of the obvious that is not seen, is reiterated in constant talk and punning, which jumps out everywhere, on eyes, vision, and visions. The hero is troubled by a burning eye within. His one current friend, in the Prologue, time present, is "a junk man I know, a man of vision," who has supplied him with wire and sockets with which to illuminate his underground—the double joke in that being that electricity is light and power and therefore vision, and that a "junk man" is a narcotics peddler, one who has visions to sell. A moment later in a marijuana sleep the hero has his first, this time surreal, vision of the facts of Negro experience. And there is more around every corner. All the novel's purpose is reiterated constantly, in fact, as its basic metaphor is elaborated: (the hero is invisible because no one sees him, and it is the function of every episode to confirm the fact that this black man is condemned to a hopeless struggle to be seen.)

The hero's end, then, is in his beginning. Quite literally. The novel happens between the Prologue and the Epilogue and those episodes constitute a single dramatic action: the hero, now, in his cellar, is doing sums in his career, writing his memoirs. And except for its burst of optimism, the Epilogue goes nowhere that the Prologue hasn't already been.[3] The novel, apparently, owes much to *Notes from the Underground*, and not least an ending that it does not clearly earn. Moreover, between the Prologue and the Epilogue, the novel moves in a series of circles—concentric planes of meaning, each traveling right back to its beginning, each mode of adventure confirming the circularity of the hero's voyaging. Each adventure is itself a repetition of each of the others and all the hero's experiences come to the same thing, but from a variety of ways of experiencing. His adventures are of a political order, and then they also have personal significances for him, having to do with his search for a personal identity, and then they are historical, marking a journey through a history of America since Emancipation which comes out where it entered, and finally they are

---

[3] Ellison says that he wrote the Prologue after he had finished the action proper of the novel.

adventures in a metaphysics, and each plane of adventuring rounds back to where it began.

(It all began, the hero says, with his grandfather, an odd old guy. He has been told he takes after him. On his deathbed his grandfather had passed on advice which, the hero says, has become a curse.

> Son, after I'm gone I want you to keep up the good fight. I never told you, but our life is a war and I have been a traitor all my born days, a spy in the enemy's country ever since I give up my gun back in the Reconstruction. Live with your head in the lion's mouth. I want you to overcome 'em with yesses, undermine 'em with grins, agree 'em to death and destruction, let 'em swoller you till they vomit or bust wide open.)

By the end of the novel the hero comes to see in his grandfather's "Yes" a greater affirmation than anything in the novel suggests his grandfather meant. He discovers in it assent to the great principles on which the country was built. But in any event, between the beginning and the ending, his grandfather's riddle defines his every gambit. The grandfather's incantatory phrases contain, Ellison has said, "a rejection of a current code and a denial become metaphysical." The hero is set earnestly to wish his way out of the curse, and the curse composes his being, his actions, and his purpose. He comes to each adventure saying Yes and he learns, or in every adventure but the last he almost learns, at the same time to say No. In the last adventure he goes underground, and it is one of the many puns brought together in that development that his "underground" is a post of constant subversion.

Between, then, his grandfather's curse in the beginning and his acceptance of it in the Epilogue, the novel moves the hero through adventures in the typical ways Negroes and whites manage, or don't manage, to live together in America. He is moved in each case to the point where all relationships disappear in an explosion, from the way of the caste system of a Southern town to that of the subtler caste system of the Negro college created and endowed by whites, the caste inherent in latter-day abolition, to that of the factory in the industrial North, to that of the dogmatic brotherliness of the Brotherhood, finally to the ultimate extension of all these ways: the race riot with which the action proper of the novel ends. And the issue of each of these adventures is a race riot of one dimension or another, and that is the point of them all. An earnest, yea-saying young man reluctant to be a saboteur explores

the typical relationships between Negroes and whites and finds
them charged with incipient violence, needing but the slightest
accident to set them off. The hero moves from one episode to another because in every one an accident happens.

The accident is always just a slight and unavoidable lapse from
the propriety he struggles to maintain. In the first episode he de-
livers his high-school valedictory address. It is a speech on the
proper subject—humility is the secret and the essence of progress
for the Negro—addressed to the Southern town's most prominent
white citizens, who are drunk at this moment and who pay no
attention to him. Benumbed by the noise, the smoke, and the reek
of the stag dinner for which he is a part of the entertainment, he
speaks the words "social equality" for "social responsibility," and
by his slip he springs from the crowd a moment of sudden, terrifying silence. In this moment of his triumph, he is crowded suddenly back into the dark, the dark from which, by his academic
prowess and his show of humility, he has thought to escape. Humility is not a technique of progress, but the means of his subju-
gation, and he dare not *not* be humble. That is something his
grandfather had known.

At college, next, with all proper respect he chauffeurs a visiting
Northern trustee, Mr. Norton. He takes Mr. Norton to a place
Mr. Norton wants to visit, the cabin of a local sharecropper, and
discovers himself in a double accident. The sharecropper tells a
story of incest and Mr. Norton suffers a heart attack. Still properly
deferential, the hero takes Mr. Norton to a local saloon, which
unfortunately this day is entertaining the Negro veterans from the
local madhouse, and he deposits him into the middle of a riot. The
adventure ends with his being expelled from college because, so
the college president tells him, he has actually obeyed the wishes
of a white man and not merely seemed to. Then in the North, as a
laborer in a paint factory, he stumbles into a union meeting and,
earnest to please everyone, he finds that because he is a Negro, he
is a scab, and as such a catalyst to violence. Then as a favored re-
cruit in the Brotherhood, he takes a single step on his own authority: he organizes a public funeral for a Brother shot by the police,
which results in the riot in Harlem that is his last adventure. It is
his one lucky accident that in that riot he tumbles into an open
manhole, leading to his coal cellar.

The lesson in his accidents is, of course, the instability in all
typical relationships between Negroes and whites in America, and
the impossibility for a Negro of propriety enough. There is always

a boomerang somewhere. Beyond that, these accidents function to reveal to the hero that he is not a person in his relations with whites, but a role, and furthermore they serve to reveal to him the kind of role he plays. It is always the same. The end of the novel is finally his ironic acceptance of his role along with his acceptance of his grandfather's curse.

His whole fate is present, though the hero is not allowed to know it, in that first adventure the climax of which is his dreadful slip of the tongue. A great part of the novel, indeed, is in that initial episode. What is revealed here is what is going to be revealed to the hero, in different circumstances, but with not much modification, in his every subsequent adventure.

In fact, in this first adventure he is clearly threatened but not actually punished for his slip of the tongue. The townsmen allow him to continue his speech, on the condition that he never forget his place. But it is his place, precisely, that the episode fixes. The scene of the speech which the hero supposes to be his valediction is itself a race riot. With some of his schoolmates, he has been made to participate in a prior entertainment for this town smoker. He and his friends are to stage a battle royal.

> We were a small tight group, clustered together, our bare upper bodies touching and shining with anticipatory sweat; while up front the big shots were becoming increasingly excited over something we still could not see. Suddenly I heard the school superintendent, who had told me to come, yell, "Bring up the shines, gentlemen! Bring up the little shines!"

They are herded before a magnificent, stark-naked blonde, and threatened if they look and threatened by the crowd if they don't. They are held there, made to suffer sexual embarrassment becoming sexual torture, and made to participate then vicariously in the lurching obscenities of the town's ranking citizens. They are goaded, threatened, tantalized, tickled, promised money, beaten, degraded and insulted, worked to the hysteria which is that of their audience, and then thrown blindfold into their battle royal where, in blind passion, they punch and kick at each other while the white mob howls around them. After the battle, at the end of their strength, they are forced to another frenzy by being made to scramble for coins on an electrified rug.

It is to this crapulous mob, in this coliseum, that the hero then talks about "social equality." The episode is a sustained orgy. It not only mocks the hero's earnest dogma of pacific humility, and it not only baptizes him in the terror that, he will find, lurks in all adventures of Negroes among American whites. There is no telling what craziness and what brutish violence lie at any next step. More than that, the episode concentrates, brilliantly, and it exposes at the pitch of a ritualistic frenzy the interior facts of caste, not only its mechanism of economic exploitation (the hero tries to make a deal with one of his schoolmates and is rebuffed, division has been effectively imposed upon them), but all its deeper exploitation of the Negro as a ritualistic scapegoat.

The hero is not only discriminated against. The politics of this system goes much deeper. In fact, he is coddled by that white man, the school superintendent, who has most immediate authority over him the school superintendent presents him for his speech with a pat on the back, a briefcase, and a scholarship. He and his schoolmates are not without honor. These whites use them in ways curiously like love. It is the function of this caste system to suppress a great deal more than the Negro, and it is the lesson of this episode that these Negroes incarnate for these whites everything that they suppress. The Negroes are made by them into the bacchants they themselves dare not be. They are made agents of, and at the same time sacrifices to, the forbidden, everything that is dark, their irrational craving for cruelty, their greed and their sex and their itch for self-destruction, the swoon of the id. These Negroes become for them, then, underground men, irrational, sinful, Satanic, the embodiment of the urgent dark, the pressing power of blackness. And beyond that, they act out for them the whole violent struggle for civilization, by first becoming the dark powers and then by exorcising themselves in violent self-punishment. And then again, in a way to triple the irony, in the same moment the Negroes justify the usage that has in the first place made them scapegoats by performing the whole of this ritual for money.

The battle royal is an extraordinarily compressed piece of work, and its one fault is that it is both more intensely maintained and more exhaustive than anything else in the novel, and so the hero's adventures hereafter become more or less adequate echoes of it. But in any event it does contain, both in its significances and in its form, the most of the hero's career. The same chaos of appetites and guilt that is the real, hidden nature of Negro and white relations is exploded at the hero in each of his subsequent accidents.

That same chaos is what is revealed in the double accident of the Mr. Norton episode. The sharecropper, upon command, *lures*

Mr. Norton to a heart attack. His story of incest has a truth of blood in it—his name is "Trueblood"—a truth that Mr. Norton, a New England gentleman and a latter-day, declined Calvinist, cannot in any other way accept. He is fascinated, as it were, into a heart attack which is the equivalent of the townsmen's orgiastic smoker. Trueblood plays out the amoral role assigned to the Negro boys of the battle royal. He does what Norton cannot do. His incest has been with his daughter, and Norton, too, has a daughter. " 'You did and are unharmed!' " Norton shouts. " 'You have looked upon chaos and are not destroyed!' " He acts out a scapegoat ritual with Trueblood and then he gives Trueblood money. Trueblood has done him some service. And the saloon episode contains the same implications, only now reversed: the Negroes use Norton for their purpose of vengeance. When he enters, the madmen go mad, and overwhelm him with the madness of blood. . . .

His reconstruction in the South having failed, having in fact collapsed into riot, the hero participates next in that next epochal event of his racial history, the Great Migration—a migration from the South to the North, the traditional road of freedom, from the country to the city, from agrarianism to industry. The Great Migration is to be another promise of progress in freedom which is not redeemed. Its end, too, is chaos bared, because it is just the same promise as that which was implicit in the liberalism of the golden day. Now that liberalism is even more distant from its source, and it has been progressively emasculated.

Fresh from his engagement with Mr. Norton, the hero comes to New York and falls upon the mercies of a young Mr. Emerson, the son of a Mr. Emerson, who has himself now become a rich New York businessman. Young, psychoanalyzed Mr. Emerson, a reader of *Totem and Taboo*, some of whose best friends are Negroes, offers the hero conspicuous kindness. He knows something about tyranny too. He considers himself his father's prisoner. He offers himself up as Huck Finn to the hero's Nigger Jim (a gesture which makes full sense, it happens, only when it is assumed that young Emerson knows about Leslie Fiedler's discovery of a homosexual theme in *Huckleberry Finn*). And young Emerson invites the hero to a party at the Club Calamus—another pale progeny, apparently, of the Golden Day.

When the hero enters industry, his paint factory, it is, as is historically appropriate, by using "Emerson's name without his permission." (Though there would seem as well to be a private joke in the event. Ralph Ellison's middle name is Waldo.) Come to industry, he discovers that the promise in the Great Migration was just a device of industrial capitalism, that he is an unwitting and certainly an unwilling weapon wielded against labor unionism, and he discovers that his coming to terms with this technological society will be nothing if not violent. The industrial war is, so far as he is concerned, just another, though a more complicated, version of the same war. The Great Migration leads him back to chaos. Specifically, the factory explosion sends him to the hospital, into, perhaps, the systematic persecutions that after World War I followed the Great Migration. It is the hospital's intent to put the hero in a glass box and render him docile. He is submitted to the equivalent of a lobotomy, which is in its turn the equivalent of another operation waggishly suggested by one of the doctors—castration. The point of the operation, a doctor explains, is that "society will suffer no traumata on his account."

The operation does not secure the intended results, and the hero is plunged then into the final one of the great events of his racial career, the Great Depression. He discovers his whereabouts by coming on what may be taken as the Great Depression's most conspicuously typical event, a tenement eviction. It is an event that provides him with another punning metaphor for his history, "dispossession," and it provides him at the same time, as is historically appropriate, with a seeming opportunity. The event is his introduction to the promising radical politics that could flourish because of such events—he makes a speech to the crowd and is on the spot recruited by the Brotherhood. There is seeming opportunity in the Brotherhood, of course, because it seems brotherly, because it is active, because it seems to make the Negro's cause its own. Beyond that, it imposes on the hero a version of his racial history that unites him with the majority, thereby eliminating the war that he has borne in his secret consciousness. The evictees for whom the hero has just spoken are, Brother Jack tells him, "agrarian types" who are being "ground up by industrial conditions," and so, all Brotherhood doctrine would seem to say, the race war is subsumed by and solved by the class war.

To wage the class war instead is not only the way toward freedom, but it is freedom itself. Like other Negro intellectuals during the Great Depression, the hero accepts this unique promise provided by the Great Depression. There is an alternative only in the futile nationalism of Marcus Garvey, for whom, in the novel, Ras the Exhorter-Destroyer stands. But then the Communist Party did not secure its promise, and so neither does the Brotherhood.

It abruptly withdraws its concerns for Harlem—and the hero comes on the fact that the race and the class wars are not identical. Furthermore, he discovers that he is bound to maintain the race war within the ranks of the Brotherhood. Brother Jack is one-eyed and cannot see him. The hero, after his first revelation of Jack's duplicity, looks around a corner of his mind and sees "Jack and Norton and Emerson emerge into one single white figure." The Brotherhood's version of history is arbitrary and does not include his history. And therefore the hero is forced back to the version of reality that at bottom he knows—which is, it turns out, Rinehart's, and which is in the image of chaos.

Rinehart is what this history comes to, and he is its hero. He is the climax of the progress up from slavery. Chaos is his freedom. He moves easily in it. He secures his living from it, and if he has been condemned to it, he takes from it also the implements of his revenge. He has made chaos a base of political action. He is a thief, a rascal, an underground man engaged in the subversion of society. Like Melville's hero, he undermines confidence, and thereby the very foundation of society.

The hero's last adventure, in the Epilogue, in his hole in the ground, serves to confirm and to deepen Rinehart, and Rinehart, the underworld man, is the last of a series of puns for the "underground" which now, in a last shift, is to become actual. The hero's progress has been a series of boomeranging reversals, and he returns now to the most final reversal of all. In every instance when he has thought he has been moving upward, he has been moving down. Especially as he has neared his last adventure there has been a play of punning foreshadowings about him all unwary. He attends the Brotherhood's social events at an apartment house named the Chthonian. He attempts to secure secret information about the Brotherhood from a girl named Sybil—as Aeneas consulted the sibyl before he entered the underworld. From the beginning his grandfather had spoken to him from the grave. The technically accommodated Negro of the paint plant had been an underground man. The Brotherhood itself is a secret, underground organization. The hero's progress has all along been a descent.

He has gone out into life repeatedly, he has been frustrated repeatedly, and at the end he descends into death. That is one implication of his drop into his underground. He has looked for definition, and found chaos. He has made a series of voyages into the world which is a white world, and he ends in the pit of darkness. He has sought rationality, and he ends in the heart of the irrational. He has looked for tranquility, and he ends in hell. There are all these suggestions brought together in his fall. His search for an adequate politics, for a technique of accommodation, his search for a personal identity, his adventuring through his own racial history, have all led him to this complete negation. The hero in his hole in the ground is back to where he began.

⋆ But his descent into the underground is the climax to still another set of implications in his adventures, and his return now to his beginnings is a full and stable resolution to all his adventures. With this final reversal, his reverses have come to an end because, like Rinehart before him, he now accepts reversal as the positive law of his being. It is his metaphysics. He is an invisible man in a world without form—but that, his underground adventure, like the Rinehart episode, goes to prove, is something. He does have an identity and a place, only they are contrary. There is a paradox in the fact that the hero's place in the world is underneath the ground, out of the world, but then the paradox is twisted again when the hero converts his hole in the ground into a home. His coal cellar, Ellison has himself pointed out, is not a sewer, but a source of heat and light and power. The hero converts all his losses to assertion. In fact he has found his politics and his person, and he has made sense out of his history, and so in his fall there is finally an ascension—which Ellison ultimately blurs by his promise that the hero will someday rise to do good among men.

His adventures have gone to prove to the hero, simply, that he is black, and, not so simply, that blackness is equivalent to the reverse of things. Now he asserts his blackness, accepting and using all its qualities and associations. The "Blackness of Blackness," the text offered by the preacher of the Prologue, has been, in effect, the text he has had to learn. In the Prologue he had said that he had to illuminate the blackness of his invisibility. Blackness is the cause of his persecution, of the deprivation of his individual humanity, of his apartness. But blackness is also the dark secrets in his persecution, all the totems and taboos that have been thrust upon him. His adventures in light and dark, in what amounts to the Manicheism of the American racial situation, have provided him with the lesson that he is Satan, whose residence should be in the underground, or as he incorporates lawlessness and irrationality he is Dionysus, or he is the darkness just behind consciousness. He is that which is hidden and deceptive and destructive, that which in nature is alien to man, invisible but present, the shadow upon the world. And he is the very principle of the boomerang which scatters all progress, all history, and all the enlightened ethics of civilization.

He embraces the *blackness* of blackness and thereby becomes an underground man—like Dostoyevski's hero, an incarnation of that which is just beneath the surface of things, that is treacherous, irresponsible, and mad.[4] He embraces that fate to which he was "before of old ordained," and thereby inherits that "power of blackness" which Melville said "derives its force from its appeals to that Calvinistic sense of Innate Depravity and Original Sin, from whose visitations, in some shape or other, no deeply thinking mind is always and wholly free."

The invisible man's end is in the embrace of his diabolism— diabolism is his politics, his identity, his history, and his metaphysics. And his future is to be Satan's—treason, violence, revenge. These are the normal activities now of his underground life. Most of the time he walks softly, he says in the Prologue, so as not to awaken the sleeping ones. He restricts himself to the subversion of Monopolated Light & Power. And he dines on his favorite dessert of vanilla ice cream and sloe gin—white, presumably, seeping blood. But once, with little direct provocation, he had beaten and almost killed a white man. An invisible man tries to make himself felt.

And the true end of the invisible man's proper adventures is in a dream of gigantic vengeance. Fallen into his coal cellar, he dreams of Jack and Emerson and Bledsoe and Norton and Ras and the school superintendent. They demand that he return to them, and when he refuses, they castrate him—they do, that is to say, what they have done. They throw his bloody parts over a bridge, but now his sex catches there, beneath the apex of the curving arch of the bridge, and drips blood into the red water. The hero laughs and tells his torturers that it is their own sun hanging

---

[4] As important a source of the hero's underground adventure would seem to be a novella by Richard Wright, "The Man Who Lived Underground," *Cross Section*, ed. Edwin Seaver (New York: L. B. Fischer, 1944), pp. 58–102. In Wright's novella, too, a Negro protagonist stumbles into an abandoned underground room which he converts to a home. Ellison's hero illuminates his cellar with 1,369 lights and he plans to have in it five radio-phonographs. Wright's hero papers the walls of his cellar with one-hundred-dollar bills, hangs the walls with gold watches and rings, and strews the floor with diamonds. Like Ellison's hero, he arranges for light by stealing electricity. Like Ellison's hero, he finds his freedom underground.

there, and their moon and their world, and that dripping upon the water is all the history they are ever going to make. And then the great bridge itself gathers itself together and slowly moves off, "striding like a robot, an iron man, whose iron legs clanged doomfully as it moved." The hero, full of sorrow and pain, shouts that it must be stopped, but that terrifying figure is his own metamorphosis. And the great dark threat in it is his resolution.

After that all messages would seem to measure Ellison's desperate reluctances. But the hero is turned, in any event, at the very end, to a staccato of abrupt affirmations—of democracy (". . . we, most of all, had to affirm the principle, the plan in whose name we had been brutalized and sacrificed"), of love (". . . in spite of all I find that I love. . . . I *have* to love"), of the mind, of social responsibility, and of the immediate prospect of his emergence. It must be said that Ellison is to be seen at the very last moment trying to take back the book he has written, or at the very least muffling all its severities, and that is unfortunate. But then it should be said as well that lacking some such attempt, there will be nothing more for Ellison ever to say.

The constant technical flaw in *Invisible Man* is that it so frequently comes to an end, and Ellison is put at every point to a greater muscularity to make the next scene more intense, more thoroughly revealing of what has already been largely revealed. It is the concomitant of that flaw that *Invisible Man* is a death-driven novel. Its movement is to confirm again and again that the hero doesn't exist, and Ellison's difficulty, to put it another way, is to resurrect the hero for each subsequent adventure. The novel's series of ironic negations is, after all, a series of negatives. It can and does reach its last possibility. Ellison will be left with only stale repetitions of the act of dying unless he can in fact assert social responsibility and mind and love—and, because the "Negro problem" is entirely an American problem, democracy. That is the only way he can keep possibility open.

That is to say that the end of *Invisible Man* is the beginning of another novel, one that will draw the complicated positive engagement of the hero in this life, specifically this American life. It is the huge achievement of *Invisible Man*, meanwhile, that it has got a vastness of experience as Negroes particularly must know it—there can be very little that it has left out—into a single meaning. The novel creates a negative metaphor, invisibility, that is fully analytic and fully inclusive, that does hold together for a moment the long experience of chaos that has met Ellison's vision.

William J. Schafer

Ralph Ellison and the Birth of the Anti-Hero

... on a farm in Vermont where I was reading *The Hero* by Lord Raglan and speculating on the nature of Negro leadership in the U.S., I wrote the first paragraph of *Invisible Man,* and was soon involved in the struggle of creating the novel.[1]

From the vantage point of the sixties, Ralph Ellison's *Invisible Man* [2] seems frighteningly prophetic. The convulsive street warfare of the last summers proves the tragic truth we have refused to face, and those episodes of the novel which may seem fantastic or morbidly hyperbolic are daily confirmed by front-page statistics. Ellison's novel, which may once have seemed limited to the special conditions of the Negro at midcentury (as a "Negro novel") is above all an *American* novel about us all, black and white together. It simply extends and develops Richard Wright's aphorism, "The Negro is America's metaphor." The riot episodes and the figure of Ras the Destroyer are no longer paper chimeras, impossible in the light of day. The cultural explosive which Ellison described in imaginative terms now shatters our cities.

The gnomic question which concludes *Invisible Man* reveals the scope of Ellison's vision: "Who knows but that, on the lower frequencies, I speak for you?" (503) This is spoken out of that tangible darkness the nameless narrator has intensified with 1,369 light bulbs, and while it is as double-edged and ironic as the rest of his story, it clearly conveys Ellison's intent. Although his story is founded in observed reality and experienced truth and Ellison answers the street cry—"Tell it like it is, baby!"—he avoids Richard Wright's bare naturalism on the one hand and James Baldwin's hypertense polemic on the other. Ellison subsumes local and temporal questions of human insight and social justice to more profound inquiries into the human mind and the justice of the heart.

Reprinted from *Critique,* X (1968), 81–93, by permission of the author. Copyright © 1968 by the author.

[1] *Writers at Work* (The *Paris Review* Interviews, Second Series) (New York, 1965), p. 328.

[2] All page references are to the paperback edition (New York, 1953).

The story is basically a quest for identity that describes America in the twentieth century—an epic journey through a labyrinth of freedom, conformity, denial and possibility. Ultimately Ellison's imagination transforms and illuminates the mingled tragedy and comedy, enslavement and freedom inherent in us all.

Technically *Invisible Man* is a *tour de force*, using a whole spectrum of fictional techniques to convey a complex authorial attitude and build a fictional world which transcends realistic description or simple probability. The action shifts from nitty-gritty realism to hallucinatory fantasy without a break in the seams of style. It is a virtuoso performance, moving from unsophisticated methods to highly complex and subtle modes of narration; Ellison especially reveals his craftsmanship in his language, which builds from colloquial idioms and maintains the rhythm and texture of speech throughout. It is an extended jazz performance—the voice used as an instrument (as in Louis Armstrong's finest work), with fluid improvisations on simple themes coalescing into a polished and organic unity.[3] But the shape of the story itself reveals Ellison's skill most clearly. The story of *Invisible Man* is fairly simple—the archetypal migration and metamorphosis of a southern rural Negro progressing to the new found land of Harlem. The tale is related by a man invisible in his impotent self-knowledge, looking back at his visible innocence—an emergent adult human looking back at the broken chrysalis.

But Ellison transforms the story into a parable, breaking with the predictable patterns of the social protest novel by blending fantasy and naturalism, moving without transition from one level of ideas to another and skillfully telescoping the episodes of the novel by concentrating closely on his protagonist's spiritual and psychological evolution. By using a relatively simple plot structure, Ellison is able to concentrate on the *quality* of the experience at hand.

The plot structure of *Invisible Man* is schematic. The novel uses a cumulative plot (in M. C. Bradbrook's illuminating terminology [4]), developing the same basic episode over and over in an emotional crescendo: the protagonist struggles idealistically to live by the commandments of his immediate social group, then is undone

---

[3] This idea is developed at length by Richard Kostelanetz, "*Invisible Man* as Symbolic History," *Chicago Review*, XIX, No. 2 (1967), 5–26.

[4] *Themes and Conventions of Elizabethan Tragedy* (Cambridge, 1960), pp. 41–42.

by the hypocrisy built into the social structure and is plunged into despair. This happens in four large movements: 1) the struggle into college, the failure with Norton and expulsion from the "paradise" of the college; 2) job-hunting in New York, Emerson's disillusioning lecture and the battle and explosion at Liberty Paints; 3) the "resurrection" or reconstruction of the protagonist, his plunge into radical activism and his purge by the Brotherhood; 4) the meeting with Rinehart, the beginning of the riots and the protagonist's confrontation and defeat of Ras, ending in the flight underground. Each episode is a development to a climax followed by a peripeteia. The novel's prologue and epilogue simply frame this series of climaxes and reversals and interpret the emotional collapse of the invisible man in the present tense. While this structure has been cited as a "technical flaw," it moves the reader from individual Negro experience to the convulsion of a whole society:

> The constant technical flaw in *Invisible Man* is that it so frequently comes to an end and Ellison is put at every point to a greater muscularity to make the next scene more intense, more thoroughly revealing of what has already been largely revealed. It is the concomitant of that flaw that *Invisible Man* is a death-driven novel. Its movement is to confirm again and again that the hero doesn't exist, and Ellison's difficulty . . . is to resurrect the hero for each subsequent adventure.[5]

This shattered effect of death, rebirth and redeath makes the novel work, illustrates completely the erasure of an individual, the process by which a man becomes invisible. The novel repeats the essential Negro experience in several ways: the overall four-part pattern might be read (albeit overly allegorically) as "emancipation," "industrialization," "organization" and "disintegration"; or the pattern may portray the violent urbanization of a rural Negro consciousness; but the linking of general Negro experience with an individual viewpoint and voice is accomplished through the repetition of the invisible man's failure and his cumulative descent into despair.

Every effect in the novel is aimed at showing the *inside* of the nameless invisible man; we are well below the skin level, and Ellison does not attempt to explain the Negro's experiences or to

---

[5] Marcus Klein, "Ralph Ellison's *Invisible Man*," in *Images of the Negro in American Literature,* ed. Seymour L. Gross and John Edward Hardy (Chicago, 1966), p. 264.

blame society for them but to show *how* he is affected, what the view is from inside the prison of blackness and invisibility. Therefore, Ellison eschews the cataloging devices of social protest fiction as well as the meticulous references to history and place—the time and place are the present landscape of the Negro mind, as it has become fused in American consciousness over 350 years. Ellison blurs the scenery to prevent the reader from absorbing the novel either in simple realistic or symbolic terms. The characters are nearly types, never probed deeply by the narrator, and the milieu is significant only insofar as it reflects and refracts the invisible man's mind.

For primarily *Invisible Man* is a study in the psychology of oppression. It is the story of an internal quest—a journey of the soul. The migration is from innocence to experience, not just from sunny south to ghetto and the underground. Ellison develops this story along mythic lines, incorporating elements of common cultural experience in the parable to generalize it further, and the protagonist's progress is finally a pilgrimage of the self. Ellison simply worked from observable American rituals:

> ... the patterns were already there in society so that all I had to do was present them in a broader context of meaning. In any society there are many rituals of situation which, for the most part, go unquestioned. They can be simple or elaborate, but they are the connective tissue between the work of art and the audience.[6]

The story, then, describes the birth of a hero—in this case, an anti-hero—retold in only slightly shaded terms; the novel is, in fact, a fragment of an epic in form.

The anti-hero of *Invisible Man*, though we come to know him intimately, remains nameless. He is no-man and everyman on a modern epic quest, driven by the message his grandfather reveals in a dream: "To Whom It May Concern ... Keep This Nigger-Boy Running." (35) His primary search is for a name—or for the self it symbolizes. During his search he is given another name by the Brotherhood, but it is no help. When he becomes a "brother," he finds that brotherhood does not clarify his inner mysteries.

In creating his anti-hero, Ellison builds on epic and mythic conventions. The nameless voyager passes through a series of ordeals or trials to demonstrate his stature. First, he passes through the initiation-rites of our society—the battle royal (exposing the

---

[6] *Writers at Work*, pp. 326–27.

sadistic sexuality of the white southern world) and speechmaking that sends him to college are parts of this rite of passage, and he is tormented into the adult world. He passes this test by demonstrating his servility and naively interpreting his grandfather's dictum: "Live with your head in the lion's mouth. I want you to overcome 'em with yeses, undermine 'em with grins, agree 'em to death and destruction, let 'em swoller you till they vomit or bust wide open." (19–20) This is the first outlook of the invisible man —the paranoia fostered by "them," the white oppressors; the boy here is Buckeye the Rabbit, the swift clever animal living by its wits beneath the jaws of the killer.

When he arrives at college, he is confronted by the deceit and duplicity of Negroes who have capitulated to a white world; he is broken by the powerful coalition of Bledsoe the Negro president and Norton the white trustee. His second trial shows him that the struggle is not a simple one of black against white, that "they" are more complex than his first experiences showed. He finds that both black and white can be turned against him.

The second phase of his career commences in the trip to New York, an exile from "paradise"; in the city, he finds Bledsoe's seven magic passports to success in the white world, the letters of recommendation, are actually betrayals, variations of the dream-letter: "Keep This Nigger-Boy Running." Thus, his primary illusions are shattered, but there are many more layers to the cocoon in which he sleeps.

For he is first of all a dreamer, a somnambulist, and sleep and dreams figure significantly in his image of himself. As he reassesses himself, his metaphor for new discoveries is the same: ". . . it was as though I had been suddenly awakened from a deep sleep." (365) Yet each sleep and each awakening (little deaths and births) prove to be interlocked layers of his existence, a set of never-ending Chinese boxes. One climactic section of the novel details his second crucial awakening—the "descent into the underworld" which occurs in chapters 10 and 11.

Like the hero of myth and ritual, Ellison's invisible man finally descends from life on the mortal plane into an underworld of death. This is the substance of the entire New York section of the novel. On arriving in the city, he recalls the plucked robin of the old song and imagines himself the victim of a fantasy-letter: "My dear Mr. Emerson . . . The Robin bearing this letter is a former student. Please hope him to death, and keep him running." (171) Then he takes the job at Liberty Paints, keeping white paint white by adding drops of pure black, under the ironic slogan, "If It's Optic White, It's The Right White" (190), which (like "If you're white, all right, if you're black, stay back") has been invented by a Negro, the ancient and malevolent Lucius Brockway. The anti-hero becomes a machine within the machines, and he finds that Brockway, an illiterate "janitor" is the heart of the whole industry. In the boiler room, an inferno, he is betrayed again by a Negro and "killed" through his treachery. But the death is the ritual death of the hero's career—a death which leads to resurrection and a new identity.

After the explosion, the anti-hero awakens in a hospital, where he is resurrected by white doctors using an electroshock machine. Chapter 11 opens with a monstrous image of the demons of this underworld: "I was sitting in a cold, white rigid chair and a man was looking at me out of a bright third eye that glowed from the center of his forehead." (202) The doctors revive him ("We're trying to get you started again. Now shut up!" [203]) to the accompaniment of fantastic effects—Beethoven motifs and a trumpet playing "The Holy City" and dreamlike dialogue from the surgeons:

> "I think I prefer surgery. And in this case especially, with this, uh . . . background. I'm not so sure that I don't believe in the effectiveness of simple prayer" (203)
>
> "The machine will produce the results of a prefrontal lobotomy . without the negative effects of the knife." (203)
> "Why not a castration, doctor?" (204)

Then, as he is revived, the doctors construct an heroic identity for him, recapitulating his existence as a Negro, starting with the first folkmyth guises of the clever Negro—Buckeye the Rabbit and Brer Rabbit: ". . . they were one and the same: 'Buckeye' when you were very young and hid yourself behind wide innocent eyes; 'Brer' when you were older." (211) The electrotherapy machine is an emblem of the mechanical society imprisoning the anti-hero: "I could no more escape than I could think of my identity. Perhaps, I thought, the two things are involved with each other. When I discover who I am, I'll be free." (212) This lesson of the resurrection is carried through the rest of the anti-hero's journey.

The apparatus which resurrects the invisible man is a mechanical womb, complete with umbilical cord attached to his stomach which is finally cut by the doctors; he is delivered of the machine, and the doctors pronounce his new name—yet he remains nameless. The doctors, who follow a "policy of enlightened humanitarianism" (215–16) declare that this New Adam will remain a social and economic victim of the machine: "You just aren't prepared for work under our industrial conditions. Later, perhaps, but not now." (215)

The anti-hero sallies forth after his revival in the underworld "overcome by a sense of alienation and hostility" when he revisits the scene of the middle class Negro arrivals in New York (223). He is now painfully aware of the hostility of his world, and he reacts not passively ("in the lion's mouth") but aggressively. In a symbolic gesture, he dumps a spittoon on a stranger whom he mistakes for his first nemesis, Bledsoe. The act is that of a crazed messiah: "You really baptized ole Rev!" (225) Then he goes forth for a harrowing of hell.

He joins the Brotherhood, an infernal organization which meets at the Chthonian club. In the Brotherhood, he rises to authority, becomes a respected leader and demagogue and is finally again betrayed by the wielders of power, whites who manipulate Negro stooges for their own ends. But at the end of this episode, the penultimate phase of the hero's career, he meets two important emblematic figures: Ras the Destroyer and Rinehart the fox. Ras, the black nationalist leader, is his crazed counterpart, and he harasses the invisible man until the night of the riots, when he attempts to hang and spear the anti-hero as a scapegoat for the mob—a dying god to appease the violence Ras releases. A contrast is Rinehart, who like Renyard is a master of deception and multiple identities: "Rine the runner and Rine the gambler and Rine the briber and Rine the lover and Rine the reverend." (430) He is a tempter, and the invisible man nearly succumbs to his temptation to freedom without responsibility; he strolls through Harlem disguised as Rinehart, the visible-invisible man who passes undetected through many identities. Ras offers the assurance of one undivided black identity and Rinehart the assurance of many shifting amoral identities—the faces of stability and flux. But the anti-hero avoids both traps, turning Ras's spear on him and shucking the dark glasses and wide hat of Rinehart, then finally dropping literally out of sight underground at the climax of the riot. Ellison has said that he took Rinehart's name from the "suggestion of inner and outer," seeming and being, and that he is an emblem of chaos—"He has lived so long with chaos that he knows how to manipulate it." [7] So Rinehart and Ras both represent chaos, two versions of disorder.

---

[7] *Ibid.*, p. 333.

Loss of identity, sleeping and blindness are the figures that express the invisible man's confusion and despair as his world disintegrates. Then, after the cultural malaise climaxes in the riot, the final phase of the anti-hero's progress begins, a descent into the tomb—the netherworld across the Styx where heroes rest: "It's a kind of death without hanging, I thought, a death alive. . . . I moved off over the black water, floating, sighing . . . sleeping invisibly." (490) So he remains immortal and waiting, like the heroes of myth who disappear and are believed to wait should the world require them—like King Arthur and Finn MacCool, sleeping giants blended into the landscape. The invisible man, now grown into Jack-the-Bear, turns to New York's sewer system, a black and labyrinthine underground—a fitting anti-hero's mausoleum.

In this black crypt he destroys his old selves one by one as he searches for light, erasing his past—burning his high school diploma, a doll which is a bitter totem of Tod Clifton's demise, the name given him by the Brotherhood, a poison-pen note, all the tokens of his identity. Then he dreams of castration and sees that the retreat has been his crucifixion—he has been cut off from the world of possibility: "Until some gang succeeds in putting the world in a strait jacket, its definition is possibility. Step outside the narrow borders of what men call reality and you step into chaos— ask Rinehart, he's a master of it—or imagination." (498) Imagination in the end redeems the anti-hero and makes his flight from battle a victory, for it gives us his story. In his tomb he is not dead but hibernating, preparing for a spring of the heart, a return which may be either death or resurrection:

> There's stench in the air, which, from this distance underground, might be the smell either of death or of spring—I hope of spring. But don't let me trick you, there *is* a death in the smell of spring and in the smell of thee as in the smell of me. (502)

The Easter of the spirit may be the emergence of the new man— no longer an anti-hero, invisible, nameless and dispossessed, but a true hero—or it may be the death of our culture.

The resurrection motif ties the story in the frame of prologue and epilogue, in the voice from underground:

> . . . don't jump to the conclusion that because I call my home a "hole" it is damp and cold like a grave; there are cold holes and warm holes. Mine is a warm hole. And remember, a bear retires to his hole for the winter and lives until spring; then he comes strolling out like the Easter chick breaking from its shell. I say all this to assure you that it is incorrect to assume that, because I'm invis-

ible and live in a hole, I am dead. I am neither dead nor in a state
of suspended animation. Call me Jack-the-Bear, for I am in a state
of hibernation. (9)

Buckeye the Rabbit has grown into the formidable Jack-the-Bear
(recalling the Bear's Son of the sagas) as the anti-hero has passed
his trials and journeyed on his downward path, reliving the recent
history of the Negro. He lies in wait beneath the inferno, under
the underworld, listening for the hero's call.

The power of *Invisible Man* comes, as I have said, not from
realistic description nor from the probability of the story but from
metaphoric or symbolic elements linking the episodes of the anti-
hero's progress. A skein of metaphor is joined with the outline of
the hero's life to unify Ellison's vision of the American dilemma.

The central metaphor is, of course, that of invisibility—light,
darkness and transparency. The novel gives shape to the inside of
invisibility—the obverse of white America's distorted mythos of
Negro life. The whites "see only my surroundings, themselves, or
figments of their imagination, everything and anything except me."
(7) Blackness and nil are the Negro's position—*nothing nowhere.*
And the novel's metaphor leads to the dilemma of identity, for the
black man cannot resign himself to nothingness or embrace invisibility: "Why, if they follow this conformity business they'll end up
by forcing me, an invisible man, to become white, which is not a
color but the lack of one." (499) Both black and white are negative; Ellison, like Melville, has used the black and white of Mani-
chaeism ambiguously so that the "power of black" is a moral consideration, not a matter of genetics or pigmentation.

A second kind of key imagery is a series of emblems of southern
Negro life invoked to describe the history of oppression since 1863.
In chapter 13, the newly resurrected anti-hero faces his mythic past
and the first demonstration of his new identity when he leads a
demonstration against an eviction. He first finds that he cannot
deny his southern heritage when he encounters a seller of Carolina
yams; the food is "forbidden fruit," because it recalls his unsophisticated country ancestry, but he eats it anyway, rebelling against
the pressure of conformity: " 'They're my birthmark,' I said, 'I
yam what I am.' " (231) Then he sees the old couple being evicted
and catalogues their possessions, which chronicle the poor Negro's
life for a century:

   . . ."knocking bones," used to accompany music at country dances,
   used in black-face minstrels . . . a straightening comb, switches of
   false hair, a curling iron . . . High John the Conqueror, the lucky

stone ... rock candy and camphor ... a small Ethiopian flag, a
faded tintype of Abraham Lincoln. ... In my hand I held three
lapsed life insurance policies with perforated seals stamped
"Void"; a yellowing newspaper portrait of a huge black man with
the caption: MARCUS GARVEY DEPORTED. ... I read:
FREE PAPERS. *Be it known to all men that my negro Primus
Provo, has been freed by me on this sixth day of August, 1859.*
(235–37)

These bits of folk myth and history permeate the novel; the invisible man, in his new aggressive role, does not renounce this culture
but embraces it, dreaming at first of flaying Bledsoe with chittlins
to humiliate him, but returning to Louis Armstrong's unanswer-
able question in the end: "What did I do/To be so black/And
blue?" As shoddy and worn as the Negro's past is, it is all that he
has, and the anti-hero embraces it in his search for identity.

Several totems the anti-hero carries on his journey link him with
his past, also. He carries the shiny briefcase awarded him after the
battle royal—a leather bribe given to buy the invisible man's
allegiance to the *status quo*. When the school superintendent presents it to him, he says, "Consider it a badge of office. Prize it. Keep
developing as you are and some day it will be filled with important
papers that will help shape the destiny of your people." (34) He
carries it as a passport into the white world of busy-ness; it seems
a sprig of moly, a talisman, but it turns out to be an albatross. In
the end it is filled only with the invisible man's cancelled identity
cards, which he burns. Thus does he find the "destiny of your
people."

Along with the briefcase he has carried homelier reminders of
his heritage—first, the fragment's of his landlady's bank:

> ... the cast-iron figure of a very black, red-lipped and wide-mouthed
> Negro, whose white eyes stared up at me from the floor, his face an
> enormous grin, his single large black hand held palm up before his
> chest. ... the kind of bank which, if a coin is placed in the hand and
> a lever pressed upon the back, will raise its arm and flip the coin into
> the grinning mouth. (277)

In a fit of rage, of reflex iconoclasm, he smashes the cliched image
of bigotry. But he feels guilty and carries the fragments with him,
unable to free himself of this shattered icon of the past. The earlier
images of chittlins and hog maws as the emblems of shame are replaced by the bank and its consolidated image of the penny-bribed
darky. With it in the briefcase is the paper dancing doll with all its

hateful connotations of the Negro who sells himself as the white man's fool. The shameful past intrudes persistently into the invisible man's present.

The imagery and the outline of the hero's life serve to give a classic shape to *Invisible Man*. If we take Joseph Campbell's summary of the hero's career as a standard, we can see how Ellison moved from reading Lord Raglan and pondering Negro leadership to the form of the novel:

> The mythological hero, setting forth from his commonday hut or castle, is lured, carried away, or else voluntarily proceeds to the threshold of adventure (exile to New York). There he encounters a shadowy presence that guards the passage (Lucius Brockway). The hero may defeat or conciliate this power and go alive into the kingdom of the dark . . . or be slain by the opposition and descend in death (the explosion and "death") . . . Beyond the threshold, then, the hero journeys through a world of unfamiliar yet strangely intimate forces, some of which severely threaten him (tests), some of which give magic aid (helpers). When he arrives at the nadir of the mythological round, he undergoes a supreme ordeal and gains his reward. The triumph may be represented as the hero's sexual union with the goddess-mother of the world [the invisible man's seduction by the white woman, who glowed "as though consciously acting a symbolic role of life and feminine fertility" (354)] . . . The final work is that of the return . . . the hero re-emerges from the kingdom of dread . . . The boom that he brings restores the world. . . .[8]

Invisible Man follows this loose form. The epic journey from southern oppression to northern invisibility is shaped by the elements of ritual hero; the anti-hero gains stature and universality by his connection with Negro folk-heroes and through his enactment of a ritual role. Only the last part of the myth is incomplete—Ellison does not decide whether the hero will emerge from underground and whether he will bring elixir or destruction. The last question of the novel is posed the reader: will it be death or spring?

Ellison, like Joseph Campbell, probes the unconscious and searches for symbolic representations for states of mind and spirit. He finds in the Negro consciousness the anxieties and problems which Campbell sees as modern man's condition; the invisible man, like all of us, faces the problem of self and other which is the shaping force behind myth:

---

[8] *The Hero With a Thousand Faces* (New York, 1949), pp. 245–46.

Man is that alien presence with whom the forces of egoism must come to terms, through whom the ego is to be crucified and resurrected, and in whose image society is to be reformed. Man, understood however not as "I" but as "Thou": for the ideals and temporal institutions of no tribe, race, continent, social class, or century, can be the measure of the inexhaustible and multifariously wonderful divine existence that is the life in all of us.[9]

The problem of identity and existence that Ellison poses transcends the issues of social justice and equity; it is not a question of "the Negro problem" or "race issues." As this novel shows in its prophecy, we must all know who we are before we can be free—and there is no freedom for a white "I" until there is freedom for a black "Thou."

[9] *Ibid.,* p. 391.

Floyd R. Horowitz

Ralph Ellison's Modern Version of Brer Bear and Brer Rabbit in *Invisible Man*

Mr. Ellison's Invisible Man is an intelligent, young Negro attuned to what he considers the clarion philosophy of the white world—"keep this nigger boy running." At first we find him like a bear, by his own admission, hibernating, unknown to anyone in a Harlem tenement basement. There he reflects upon his past experience, which soon, like Dante's travail to the blinding light of knowledge, is to be recounted. We can meanwhile understand

Reprinted from *Midcontinent American Studies Journal,* IV (1963), 21–27, by permission of the author and the journal. Copyright © 1963 by *Midcontinent American Studies Journal.*

symbolically one of his preoccupations. Around him in this dark basement he has rigged electric fixtures. He has tapped a power line and currently is stealing the electricity that illuminates his hibernation. On the ceiling and walls there are now 1369 lighted bulbs. Such enlightenment metaphorically sets the tone of the book. It is from one frame of reference a psychological study, impressionistically told.

So begins the story. In the South, once, a Negro boy was awarded by the whites a scholarship to a Negro state college. He was to learn the tradition of Booker T. Washington—practical service to the Negro community, humble dignity (at least in public), intellectualized acceptance of white authority. And naively on that foundation he frames his goals, and affixes in the rafters the hopeful branch of religion. Dilligently and in innocence he learns to conform. As a reward, in his third year, he is chosen to chauffeur a visiting white trustee of the college.

The day is a disaster. Taking a back road he allows the delicately sensitive trustee to see the Negro in all his squalor. Following a conversation with a farmer who is known to have committed incest, the trustee faints and is carried to the only available haven, a saloon and brothel just then at the height of its weekly business with the Negro ambulatory Vets of a mental institution. Within the day our hero is dismissed from the college of conformity, on the morrow traveling North to the expectation of greater freedom.

In short order, thus upon the verge of manhood, other disillusionments follow. The letters of recommendation which he carries from the college president prove treacherous. In the North he is economically exploited. Because of his skill as a public speaker he is enlisted by the Communists and later duped. In the shadow of each rebuff he distinguishes his grandfather's enigmatic smile and hears his words: "overcome 'em with yesses." Accordingly, the race of his experience in the South and North exhausts his consciousness of self. He finds that in running he is nowhere. Like a continually endangered Odysseus under the polyphemal white eye of society he is Noman. The whites are blind to him, he is invisible to himself, having failed in a succession of roles. While in itself this is a kind of knowledge by suffering, it is more than he can bear. His self-imposed basement exile is therefore an escape from responsibility, if also from the inequity of a hostile world. The winter of his discontent, he knows, must come to its hibernative end, and he must chance the new spring, yet for the time—and for the emphasis of the novel—his past disillusioning experience must be narrated.

Because the mode of that narration is impressionistic, Ellison takes the opportunity to convey the largest part of the novel's meaning via a quite imaginative, often bizarre range of imagery. In that way the logic of image associations sets out the basis of thematic implication. This may come as a new idea to the historian and litterateur alike, especially because the social and political significance of Mr. Ellison's book seems conclusively to derive from its open drama, colorful vignettes, and frank appraisals. Yet it may not be amiss to demonstrate that there is a good deal more social and political commentary being effected in the work via a highly planned if somewhat covert structure.

This means several things. Such a demonstration is necessarily involved with its own tools, the logic of interpolation as well as the more generally understood judgement of interpretation. Further, the story is not always told literally, but rather is rendered by symbols and images that have something like a life of their own. At an extreme (the Invisible Man's experience while in shock), the literal result takes the form of an impenetrable impressionistic morass, and the reader must agree to witness rather than to understand in the traditional sense. Other times a logical association can be drawn from similar instances: at the beginning of the novel the Invisible Man comes to a southern "smoker" where he will enter the prize-fight ring, and while there he sees a nude dancer who has an American flag tattooed on her belly: at the end of the book he is described as a "black bruiser" who is "on the ropes" and "punch drunk" and he scrawls another distortion of another American message across the belly of another nude: "Sybil, you were raped/ by/ Santa Claus/ Surprise." Such devices as these form the texture (albeit an ironic one) of the American meanings which the hero experiences, and which no less importantly the reader is invited to experience with him.

As we do so we may trace the Invisible Man as a Christ-like figure, sacrificed and sacrificing. Many of the symbols by which he is described are distinctly Christian symbols, many of his actions are analogues of Biblical events. Or, psychologically considered, he is the dramatic vortex of Negro neuroticism: so extensive is the imagery here that we must read and interpret with the aid of an unabridged Freud. Historically and politically, too, he is beset by a cavalcade of American symbols and images which are in the wrong places, a sometimes subtle, sometimes raucous debunking of the names and institutions which Americans are supposed to hold so dear: the American flag upon her belly undulates to the shimmy of a nude, the identity of Jefferson is an illusion in the mind of a shell shocked veteran, the Statue of Liberty is obscured in fog while liberty is the name appellate to a corporate enterprise, Emerson is a businessman, the Fourth of July is Jack the Communist's birthday as well as the occasion of a race riot.

Based fairly closely upon the folklore motif of Brer Rabbit and Brer Bear, the line of imagery discussed in this paper is as ironic as such other patterns of meaning, and perhaps even more so because of its Negro origin. Like the novel's fifty or perhaps seventy-five other motifs, it is not especially extensive, nor does it so closely effect an analogy that it admits of no other meaning for its individual parts. Quite the opposite. The bear and the rabbit are sometimes psychologically one in the same, as in Jack the Rabbit, Jack the Bear. But it would seem that the rabbit can be Peter as well. Or he is called Buckeye, which describes Jack the Communist later on. Or he is about to be peppered with BUCKshot. Or there is a pun on bear, so that the hero can not bear his existence. There is, in short, a rich language play which intertwines this motif with many others, which, perhaps too gratuitously on occasion, identifies rabbit with Brer Rabbit, which makes literary explication not the easiest of pursuits. Yet, for all that, the point of Ellison's use of this motif seems plain enough. Though they are sometimes friendly enough, less than kin and more than herbiverous quadrupeds, rabbit and bear are naturally irreconcilable. More, we know from Uncle Remus that soon they will match wits.

This makes for a good metaphor in which to cast the Invisible Man, since, interestingly enough, for Ellison, wit is not the same as intelligence. His protagonist is not a victor. Early in his education the Invisible Man discovers that. While he is chauffeuring Mr. Norton, the trustee of the college, they approach Jim Trueblood's back road shack. The Invisible Man mentions that Trueblood has had relations with his own daughter. Norton demands that the car be stopped. He runs over to Trueblood, accosts him, wants his story. While the amazed and morally upright Invisible Man looks on, Trueblood complies in full detail. Ellison already has described him "as one who told the old stories with a sense of humor and a magic that made them come alive." And again, as one "who made high plaintively animal sounds." Now this story: sleeping three abed because of the extreme cold, his wife, daughter and himself, as if in a dream well beyond his control, just naturally, incest occurred. The story is a colloquial poetic. Before the act Trueblood has been nothing, but now he freely admits: "But what I don't understand is how I done the worst thing a man can do in his own family and 'stead of things gittin bad, they got better. The nigguhs up at the school don't like me, but the white folks treats me fine."

This irony is the key to Ellison's entire treatment of Brer Rabbit and Brer Bear's relationship. Here the issue is moral. Trueblood, in the middle of the night which he describes "Black as the middle of a bucket of tar," has given his daughter a baby. For this he is rewarded. Norton gives him a hundred-dollar bill. "You bastard," says the Invisible Man under his breath, "You no-good bastard! You get a hundred-dollar bill!" Playing the bear, the Invisible Man is fooled, of course; thrown out of school in a hurry. In vain he objects to the college president: "But I was only driving him, sir. I only stopped there after he ordered me to. . . ." "Ordered you?" retorts the president, "He *ordered* you. Dammit, white folk are always giving orders, it's a habit with them. Why didn't you make an excuse? Couldn't you say they had sickness—smallpox—or picked another cabin? Why that Trueblood shack? My God, boy! You're black and living in the South—did you forget how to lie?"

This is the form of the anecdote. Brer Bear is outwitted by Brer Rabbit in a first encounter. So the Invisible Man travels to the North. There on the streets of New York City he meets the second rabbit man, in this instance named Peter. Of course, exactly considered, Peter Rabbit is not the same as Brer Rabbit, yet he belongs to the same tradition. He knows how to escape the McGregors of the world. Here in Harlem he looks like a clown in baggy pants, wheeling a cart full of unused blueprints. Says Peter, "Man, this Harlem ain't nothing but a bear's den." The Invisible Man then completes the bridge of logic to the original analogy: "I tried to think of some saying about bears to reply, but remembered only Jack the Rabbit, Jack the Bear." Peter needs no social reenforcement, however. He proffers his key to success: "All it takes to get along in this here man's town is a little shit, grit, and mother-wit. And man, I was bawn with all three." So the friendly side of the rabbit's personality, advising the Invisible Man what to expect from the city, the North, the white world. But it is no use, for the bear must always be tricked—and soon he is.

He has heard of a job at Liberty Paints and hurried to apply. The scene depicts a patriotic devotion to the free enterprise system: flags flutter from the building tops. A screaming eagle is the company's trade mark. Liberty Paints covers America with what is advertised as the whitest white possible, a defective shipment just then being sent out for a Washington national monument. The bear is sent down, down, down, to help the irascible Negro, Lucius Brockway.

"Three levels underground I pushed upon a heavy metal door marked 'Danger' and descended into a noisy, dimly lit room. There was something familiar about the fumes that filled the air and I had just thought *pine*, when a high-pitched Negro voice rang out above the machine sounds." In an image which we may recall, the first rabbit, Trueblood, has already dreamed of such machinery. And his black as tar description is taken up now by the Invisible Man's thought of *pine*, and by Ellison's pun "high-pitched." So the hero encounters Lucius, the next Brer Rabbit, who is described as small, wiry, with cottony white hair, who defends himself by biting, and whose coveralls covered by goo bring the image of the Tar Baby to the Invisible Man's mind.

Against Lucius's grit and mother-wit there is barely any defense. It turns out that Lucius alone has the secret of America's whitest white paint. He and no one else knows the location of every pipe, switch, cable and wire in the basement heart of the plant. Only he knows how to keep the paint from bleeding (whereas Trueblood does actually bleed for his moral smear), only he how to mix the base. He has helped Sparland, the big boss, word the slogan "If it's Optic White, It's the Right White." And he knows his worth: "caint a single doggone drop of paint move out of the factory lessen it comes through Lucius Brockway's hands." So in the matter of economics as before with morals, Brer Bear cannot win. As Lucius's assistant he tends the steam values, and when they pass the danger mark, burst, Brockway scrambles for the door and escapes while the Invisible Man attempts to shut them off and is caught in the steam. Again we may remind ourselves that the concepts of machinery and scalding have been united in Trueblood the rabbit's dream. Brer Bear can not win no matter how hard he tries.

In this case, moreover, his efforts are naive, short of the hypocrisy which alone means survival for the natively talented Negro. While he struggles for consciousness and self in the company hospital, that fact of Negro existence is brought out. A card is placed before him: "What is your name?" Under the bludgeoning of experience he has lost his identity, "I realized that I no longer knew my own name. I shut my eyes and shook my head with sorrow." The fantasy of his impression continues. Other cards are submitted, finally the question: "Boy, who was Brer Rabbit?" Soon after he is released in a daze, finds his way to Harlem and collapses on the sidewalk.

Here Ellison has been portraying the New Negro intellectual. What has this Invisible Man learned?—that in the South, in the course of enlightenment he is pitted against his fellow Negro, farmer and college president alike; that Negro inured to the quasi-slavery practiced by the white. And in the North little better: survival in a slum, a bear in a bear den. Yet defeat is a realization, and a realization is a victory of perspective. In short, he is no simple Brer Bear. It is Ellison's intention to have him learn what the young intellectuals must learn—that as long as narrow self interest motivates him he can have no peace. His must be the realm of the universal. That becomes the next phase, not with a rush of empathy, but as before, through trial, through defeat, through knowledge of self.

One day, when he has recovered from his ordeal in the paint factory, he comes upon the Harlem eviction of an aged Negro couple. Their meagre possessions on the sidewalk, the wife attempts to return into their apartment to pray. When the marshals in charge refuse permission the crowd riots. Suddenly in the melee the Invisible Man hears himself yelling, "Black men! Brothers! Black Brothers!" His further role as Brer Bear has begun. Under the aegis of his colloquial eloquence the crowd returns the furniture to the apartment. Then, in another moment, the police have arrived and he searches for a way of escape. A white girl standing in the doorway accosts him, "Brother, that was quite a speech you made," directs him to the roof. He hurries across to another building, down the stairs, into the street a block away, across to a far corner. But as he waits for the light to change there comes the quiet, penetrating voice beside his ear, "That was a masterful bit of persuasion, brother." The biggest, most persistent rabbit of all has just tracked him, Brer Jack the Communist, alias Buckeye the one-eyed international hopper. Brer Bear is wanted for the organization. Will he listen over coffee?

Says the Invisible Man, "I watched him going across the floor with a bouncy rolling step." Again: "His movements were those of a lively small animal." And Jack's pitch is short: "Perhaps you would be interested in working for us. We need a good speaker for this district. Someone who can articulate the grievances of the people. They exist, and when the cry of protest is sounded, there are those who will hear it and act." Communism is the answer to his needs, for as many reasons as it is advertised to have. It offers him a cause, social equality and a job. It fulfils what must seem the generic destiny of a Brer.

What informs the Communist policy is the scientific attitude, however, not the man but the mass. To this positivistic philosophy the Invisible Man must immediately be trained, for in the course of change to the new brotherhood, he is told by Hambro the Communist philosophe, certain sentimental ideas will have to be sacrificed. The very idea of race, that core and defense of Negro unity, must be sublimated. Nor is there place in the Brotherhood's teaching for emotion, for psalm singing, yam-eating, Tuskeegee zeal. All is to be logical: the answers to the woman question, the rational youth groups, the organization of labor, even the public rallies. At least this is the theory, and if like Liberty Paints it is myopic and actually tinged with grey, if the women take him to bed to answer their political questions, if the youth are too easily frantic, if the public is still strong for the gospel and labor distrusts the Negro as scab; if these realities, the Invisible Man's idealism draws him into the bear trap, Brother Jack his foil.

His *is* a persuasive skill. Soon he is known, liked, trusted, powerful, confident that the Brotherhood is leading the Negro aright. Now he is willing to fight Ras the Exhorter, leader of the Negro-only movement. But as quickly, the trap springs: the internationally directed Brotherhood changes its Harlem policy. Indefinitely, there will be an interdiction of its plan to better the Negro's social condition. Unless the Invisible Man is willing to sacrifice the trust, the hopes of his fellow Negro, he must renounce identity once more.

In a scene which proves the Brotherhood's shortsightedness— Brer Jack, it turns out, actually has but one eye—there comes the break. But now, unallied, the Invisible Man must reckon with Ras the Destroyer, who in a Fourth of July flash electrifies Harlem as the nationalist leader of a super race riot. This is no time for intellectualism, nor this the place. Pursued, to survive, our hero has no choice but to hide in an underground cavern. There we find him when the novel begins: "Call me Jack-the-Bear, for I am in a state of hibernation." That is the pattern, from rural copse to cosmopolitan forest.

5. Suggestions for Study

Stewart Rodnon

Ralph Ellison's *Invisible Man:* Six Tentative Approaches

The need to solve the crucial and intensifying problem of the Negro's status in American life has an urgency which commands the attention of most of us. For the teacher of English any novel which deals with Negro-White relationships in a sensitive and intelligent manner rates immediate priority; when such a novel wins the National Book Award (in 1952) and when a poll of two hundred editors, authors and critics results in its being declared the most significant work of fiction to be published by an American since World War II, then certainly Ralph Ellison's *Invisible Man* [1] demands and deserves widespread dissemination, especially among our younger citizens.

To aid in the examination of this novel, I am offering in the following pages some critical commentary concerning its virtues, which can serve as a guide line for establishing its reputation; in addition to developing briefly six possible approaches for presenting this novel to the student, I shall explore in more depth one of these approaches—the novel's relation to other works in American literature—in order to demonstrate how any of the other five may be developed.

Of the many auditors who have praised the novel, two have been especially articulate in its behalf; F. W. Dupee declared *Invisible Man* a "veritable *Moby Dick* of the racial crisis" and "a distinguished contribution to literature" which admirably fulfilled its aim of humanizing the Negro by demonstrating that his cultural accomplishments could be linked "with the history, lore, and art of mankind at large." [2] And Robert Bone, in his comprehensive *The Negro Novel in America*, insisted that Ellison was "a writer of the first-magnitude," a creative intellect whose unique talent revealed

---

Reprinted from the *College Language Association Journal*, XII (1969), 244–56, by permission of the author and the College Language Association. Copyright © 1969 by the College Language Association.

[1] Available in paperback as Signet T-1823, published by the New American Library.

[2] "On *Invisible Man,*" *Book Week* (September 26, 1965), p. 4.

itself in a personal idiom composed of "fantasy, distortion, and burlesque." [3] Further, Bone declares that Ellison "penetrates to the heart of the two great illusions of his time" for *Invisible Man* is based on a sophisticated understanding of modern political science. The novel is a superb chronicle both of "the shibboleths of American capitalism—a social system which he apprehends through the institutional structure of the Southern Negro college" and the fraudulent attitudes of "Stalinism, which he encounters through a revolutionary organization known as the Brotherhood" (p. 197). By structuring his novel about each of these two disillusionments, Ellison has produced a first-rate socio-political document as well as an important work of literary art.

A novel which has garnered such praise and sympathetic understanding must contain riches of many kinds. Precisely because it has these riches of sources, technique, characterization and theme, it becomes an eminently teachable novel. A first approach could be its relationship to, and its dependence on, classic and contemporary literature in America. Since I wish to develop this approach more fully in a later section of this article, I shall merely indicate here the possibility that the novel may be associated with the work of at least a dozen figures from Herman Melville to Saul Bellow.

A second approach would be its relationship to some of the classics of Western civilization. One book which affords immediate comparison is Dostoevsky's *Notes From Underground*. Several critics have commented on the parallels: in both books we have an exploration of the lower depths of human personality, both question the nature of reality and meaning of social responsibility, and both explore the limits of human possibility. The two authors, moreover, share a central concern with individuality, with that which enables man to insist upon the value of the uniqueness of his existence in the face of all established systems. To do this each protagonist withdraws from human contact into an underground cave to seek a haven in which he can hibernate in order to re-group his psychic forces. Until each learns the significance of sympathy and human brotherhood, the plague-ridden protagonist must, as Camus' Dr. Rieux suggests, "do what one has to do" when faced with adversity. Pursuing this motif of alienation, one could compare the nightmare scenes, e.g., the Harlem race riot, of *Invisible Man* with the similar surrealistic quality of Franz Kafka's fictional world, particularly with *The Trial* and with *Metamor-*

---

[3] (New Haven, 1965), p. 196.

phosis. To swing the pendulum to its opposite extreme, one might emphasize the novel's rich comic elements; surely Ellison's portrait of the hypocritical Bledsoe begs for comparison with some of Charles Dickens' larger-than-life delineations of Establishment characters; one could sustain, through this avenue of approach, the idea of exaggeration as a mode of satire. Finally, excerpts from James Joyce's *Ulysses* might be cited as affording meaningful comparisons on the comic level, especially in each author's manipulation of mythic elements.

Dealing with the purely literary qualities of the novel is a third approach; in using this strategy, one could subsume at least six areas for development. First, Ellison's humor is shrewd and all-embracing. Discussing American humor as a base—Constance Rourke's *American Humor* and Walter Blair's *Native American Humor* would be invaluable adjuncts—one could point out the wide range of Ellison's techniques of humor, a comic spirit which ranges from boisterous slapstick to incisive, controlled ironic commentary on the action of the moment. Secondly, the Gothic quality of the novel could be examined; the history and the nature of Gothic could serve as a cohesive force for a discussion of such nightmare, surrealistic scenes as the one in the men's smoker, the Liberty Paint episode, and, especially, the race-riot description which concludes the second major section of the novel. Offering a third approach is the use of metaphor. The metaphoric richness of *Invisible Man*—the title itself a metaphor—especially that of light vs. dark would sustain a careful examination, for the pictorial foundation serves to reinforce the novel's essential thematic content. A fourth method of examination might focus on the sustained point of view maintained by the novelist. The "I" narrator, i.e., a Negro who considers that to the white man he is invisible, maintains an esthetic distance from the reader not only because he is telling the story from a retrospective position, but also because as an articulate and intelligently ironic observer he can demonstrate his dramatic immersion in life while he simultaneously examines the meanings of his experiences in a detached, cool attitude. The richness and raciness of the prose offer a fifth avenue of examination. Ellison's superb control in handling Negro speech patterns, his close study of and evident relish for jazz rhythms, and his scholarly, alert perusal of contemporary slang suggest wide possibilities for discussion, among them the use of colloquially "real" language as a heritage of the American novel at least since the work of the local colorists and Mark Twain, or an analysis of contemporary slang along more theoretical lines. The prevalence of mythic elements in the conversation and exposition of the novel suggests a sixth view; one might use Erich Fromm's definition of myth as "a message from ourselves to ourselves" as the basis for a discussion of Negro folk mythology. The whole strategy of the novel, for example, reminds one of the positioning of the Negro in his folk tales as the underdog who somehow manages to outwit the superior strength of a more powerful adversary. This natural tendency, reflecting sociological and psychological truths, could also be tied to the "trickster" motif, especially evident in the Rinehart segment of *Invisible Man;* this idea could be developed extensively, with parallels traced back almost to the earliest of written records.

The fourth major approach to the teaching of the novel is through an analysis of its themes; at least three thematic strands lend themselves to intensive investigation. Sensitive literary artists in America have devoted themselves to examining and attacking many areas of American life, generally focusing upon that character who observes with distaste, or himself demonstrates, a selling out to the Establishment. In his depth analysis of the hypocritical Bledsoe—whose pietism masks his power drive and whose preaching of the ideal of Negro docility and slow melioration is an acceptance of the conservative white man's view of black improvement—and in his view of Norton and other "successful" white men, Ellison strikes incisively not only at the status-quo platitudes of the conservative power-elite but also at the pseudo-liberal who uses his money to relieve his sense of guilt concerning the Negro's second-class status in America. A second thematic line, and one which offers a wider range of implications, is that of Negro-White relations. To understand the causes of the long, hot summer explosions in Harlem and Bedford-Stuyvesant in 1964, Watts in 1965, Chicago and Cleveland in 1966 and Detroit and Newark in 1967, the average American needs—in addition to demanding the obvious panacea of increased Federal funding—an increased awareness of the Negro's view of his condition. Ellison, far more than a "Negro" writer, brings an artistic consciousness to bear on his life and times. In his novel he analyzes and deciphers the complex relationships among Whites and Negroes; he moves beyond either the stereotypes of racist spokesmen or the Negrophilia of professional liberals to an intelligent, sane and telling awareness of what it means to be black in White America. Finally, the novel develops the thematic line of progressive disillusionment which is, perhaps, a form of education

—or maturity. We have presented here the classic initiation into evil or, in another way, the education from innocence to awareness. Here, the betrayals by Bledsoe and, later, the Brotherhood are psychic insults to the narrator and ultimately force him to his cellar-haven to make a synthesizing review of his experiences. This underground retreat-of-the-mind is basically a hibernation in which the protagonist is preparing for future action; as he says, "a hibernation is a covert preparation for a more overt action" (p. 16).

A fifth major approach could focus upon a comparison of *Invisible Man* to other novels of a special pattern. The volume bears resemblances to such *bildungsroman* as *Huckleberry Finn, The Way of All Flesh,* Faulkner's *The Unvanquished, In Our Time, The Catcher in the Rye* among dozens of possible choices. It is similar to such works of self-discovery as *A Separate Peace, Herzog,* and *Rabbit, Run.* It may be examined as one more of the sensitive-individual's-reaction-to-a-mass-society novel; in praise of the individual, it satirizes many facets of our culture and bears this resemblance to such works as *Main Street, On the Road* and *The Winter of Our Discontent.* One might note too, that the novel fits the anti-hero concept. Here, the "I" of *Invisible Man* insists, despite temporary social defeat and psychological abuse, on his personal integrity and personal worth. Because of this existential overtone, a whole spectrum of modern authors could be cited for valid comparison: several of Sartre's central figures, Camus' protagonists, Bellow's questing idealists, Malamud's "sad and bitter clowns," [4] and Philip Roth's sardonic narrators.

Although the sixth approach to the teaching of *Invisible Man* is probably the most obvious, it might offer the widest teaching rewards. By pegging the novel directly to the White-Negro experiences of the student, one could develop general class discussion of prevalent attitudes toward the Negro and how this novel either reinforces or counters these attitudes. Panels could be formed, too, to discover the validity or the fallacies of Ellison's views; debates could be arranged as a base from which the novel could be discussed. Obvious written assignments based on the student's reading of the novel come immediately to mind; these could range from simple reaction reports to the book through personal essays dealing with the race problem and might conceivably diverge into ex-

---

[4] Part of the title of Bernard Siegel's article in *Northwest Review,* V (Spring, 1962), 69–80.

pository prose statements in such sub-areas as the conformity-vs.-individualism motif and the relation of the Negro to "the American Dream."

Because of the essentially sketchy nature of the six approaches developed above, it seems appropriate here to focus on one of them —the relation of the novel to that prose usually examined in the traditional American Literature survey—and to examine it more fully as a guide to how each of the other six might be developed. To deal with all the possibilities, even in this one approach, would require a volume, and therefore it hardly needs to be stated that the following exploration is at best a tentative evaluation of only a small percentage of the potentially useful literary works.

In *Shadow and Act*,[5] his brilliant miscellanea published in 1964, Ellison reveals a highly sophisticated grasp of American classical literature, especially in the two pieces "Twentieth-Century Fiction and the Black Mask of Humanity" and "Stephen Crane and the Mainstream of American Fiction." As well, he demonstrates a wide and deep reading of European literature which has earned him the accurate accolade as "a man of letters who has written a novel." For Ralph Waldo Ellison, the crucial sources for his novel seem to lie among classic American writers, possibly beginning with Benjamin Franklin as a lesser influence—note the shrewd common sense attitudes of several characters and the use of "Poor Richard" aphorisms which dot the novel—through the major seminal sources which include the more important Transcendentalists. At least he certainly mirrors the latter's Romantic preoccupation with the intrinsic worth of the individual, the value of personal integrity, and the unifying idea of the brotherhood of man. While it is unnecessary to demonstrate here these ideas as they occur in the work of Emerson and Thoreau, they may be clearly observed in *Invisible Man* in the grandfather motif, the affirmation of selfhood by the protagonist, and the quietly desperate battle against major stifling forces such as the false American dream as it affects the Negro and the fake optimistic idealism of the Brotherhood.

One might project the thesis that even more influential than the essays of Emerson and Thoreau are the novels of Herman Melville, whose view of the Transcendentalists was less than complimentary. As previously noted, Dupee has contended that Ellison's novel is the *Moby Dick* of the race issue, with "the terrors and exaltations

---

[5] Available in paperback as Signet Q-3022, published by the New American Library.

of Negro-White existence replacing those of the whaling voyage":
in it "the hero's search for a real identity and human function"
supplants the chase after Moby Dick.[6] He could with equal justification develop the whole appearance-vs.-reality parallel which
runs through all of Melville's novels. The great "strike through the
mask" chapter of Melville's masterpiece and his use of the whole
concept of masks in *The Confidence Man* and, to a lesser degree,
in *Pierre* have been examined adequately by several auditors; the
"Rinehart" section of *Invisible Man* particularly offers parallel
thematic and artistic comparisons. The relation to *Pierre* might
be sustained not only by each author's handling of incest situations, but also by noting the tortured existence of each central
character. Melville's *Benito Cereno*, itself the object of widespread
critical scrutiny, might serve as a parallel; Captain Amasa De-
lano's obtuse and almost willful lack of perception of the Negro
mirrors the essential attitude of most White Americans, according
to Ellison's view.

Among the early Romantics, Poe and Whitman probably offer
the most obvious and fruitful comparisons. Surely the surrealism,
the horror and the power of blackness which dominate most of
Poe's tales may be juxtaposed with both the nightmare re-birth
scene at the factory hospital and the view of the Harlem race riots.
Moreover, an examination of the careful architecture and the sustained imagery base of Ellison's novel plus a reading of Poe's "The
Philosophy of Composition" could draw classroom discussion to
the problems of the artist as craftsman. With Whitman, the obvious affinity is with the central motif of "Song of Myself"; the
artist's concern with the question of identity. Ellison's novel and
Whitman's poem may be examined in an attempt to show how the
problem of man's relation to society and to the universe was developed by a Romantic poet in the middle of the nineteenth century and how it was handled by a novelist some one hundred years
later. On the other hand, one could pursue the Whitmanesque idea
of the primitive, an attitude in which the Negro becomes the exemplar of the Noble Savage, and which leads to a dangerously
oversimplified and distorted view of the Negro's place in American
life.

Viewing post-Civil War literature, one discovers deeper affinities
between Ellison's novel and those volumes published during the
chastening decades prior to World War 1. Particularly do the writ-

---

[6] Dupee, p. 4.

ings of Samuel Clemens and Henry Adams offer some mordant and incisive parallels. Most useful in comparing the Clemens-Ellison relationship are two significant novels of the earlier writer, *Huckleberry Finn* and *Pudd'nhead Wilson*. In addition to employing the obvious stylistic devise of using a sustained "I" character who tells his story in retrospect, *Huckleberry Finn* and *Invisible Man* have at least four other similarities: the essential theme that basic human values are more important than transient social mores, the "education" of a young central character, the journey motif (both external and internal), and the rich use of Negro folk material. With *Pudd'nhead Wilson* one could demonstrate the common dilemmas of appearance vs. reality, of public opinion vs. individual insight. Examining the tragic waste in the life of Chambers Driscoll and of "Pudd'nhead" Wilson, one may see a parallel to that situation which today engulfs the potential of the American Negro. On the other hand, the patrician society of Brahmin Boston seems about as distant a social stratum as one might imagine. Yet binding *The Education of Henry Adams* to *Invisible Man* is an idea of "education" to life. Paradoxically, Henry Adams' formal education, probably the finest available to an American of his generation, couldn't prepare him for the rough-and-tumble, devil-take-the-hindmost civilization of the Gilded Age. His education led him, in a general sense, to the defeat of his idealism. It is there that one comes upon the essential similarity of the two books: one sees two variations of the often-told story of the sensitive and intelligent young man discovering that if he strikes through the mask, if he tears off the veneer, if he strips the gilding, what he discovers is an essentially corrupt and Mammon-seeking society, which protects itself with rationalizations and hypocrisies. The young man, learning this bitterest of lessons, is left to face the awareness that most of his ideals will have to be lost, for life in its inexorable sequence is a process of progressive disillusionment.

Moving to the literature between the two World Wars, possibly the works best suited to discussion would be the prose of Hemingway and Faulkner and the poetry of T. S. Eliot. Although Ellison has avoided the Hemingway style, his novel surely may be compared to *In Our Time*. The closest immediate resemblance is in the initiation theme; just as Hemingway has Nick Adams meet several emotional and physical crises, so too does Ellison's protagonist face a series of incidents which are physically maiming, e.g., the explosion in the paint factory, and psychically injurious, e.g., the Bledsoe betrayal. In each book the major figure ends severely scarred, but is viable enough to make a therapeutic retreat from civilization; this concluding experience in each case suggests that the protagonist will return, although chastened and disillusioned, after a period of psychic regeneration. Another of Hemingway's ideas which could be emphasized is the use of the Negro as exemplar of primitivism. In Hemingway's work Negroes rarely appear. When they do, however, they tend to reinforce the primitive line of the novel or story: in *The Sun Also Rises*, Bill Gorton's comments on the Negro prizefighter in Vienna fall into place beside the other allusions to sports, for skill, courage and endurance are the cardinal virtues; in *The Battler*, Ad Francis is kept manageable by his Negro "protector," Bugs; in *The Killers*, Sam, the Negro cook, offers young Nick Adams the gutter-sharp philosophy of non-involvement in a potentially dangerous situation.

The work of William Faulkner contains so much more material concerning the Negro that it is impossible here to do more than suggest several of the myriad possibilities. The work of Faulkner and Hemingway seems to have as a common base the idea of primitivism, probably the result of their own pleasure in the sport of hunting and fishing and to the impact of Freudian ideas of the unrepressed and "adjusted" man who is closest to nature. This attitude toward the primitive probably colors the best statement of Faulkner's concerning the Negro; in *The Bear* Ike McCaslin explains why he relinquishes the land which is legally his, and in his repudiation of the past of the South, he offers a beautifully wrought statement concerning the virtues of the Negro, emphasizing his endurance, forbearance, pity and fidelity. Additionally, one may find in examining the whole body of Faulkner's work that Negroes usually are a stabilizing, enduring and positive force. They are a few dark fragments which Faulkner shores against the ruins of the collapsing Southern aristocracy, and offer, as Robert Frost has stated about a poem, "a momentary stay against confusion."

At least six other Faulkner volumes might be examined for their attitudes toward the Negro, and, therefore, might offer fruitful areas for discussion of the Ellison novel: *The Sound and the Fury; Light in August; Absalom, Absalom!; The Unvanquished; Go Down, Moses*, and *Intruder in the Dust*. In comparing *Invisible Man* to each of these, one might note the similar treatment of incest in *The Sound and the Fury;* also one could develop the resemblances between the maternal Mary Rambo of *Invisible Man* and Dilsey Gibson's role as a member of the Compson household.

For *Light in August* the most obvious parallel is between the tortured flight of Joe Christmas, the stranger who searches for a place in an alien society, and the geographical flight of Ellison's protagonist from South to North. For *Absalom, Absalom!*, probably Faulkner's most stylistically difficult novel, one could examine the Southern White attitude just prior to and following the Civil War. The harshness of attitude in that volume is partially vitiated by Faulkner's *The Unvanquished* which, dealing with much the same period, presents an almost stereotyped view of a young White boy and a Negro slave boy being brought up together. Here, too, we are given some insight into the White boy's gradual awareness of, and changing attitudes toward, the Negro. *Go Down, Moses* sweeps historically through several generations of the White and Negro McCaslins; although less valuable in dealing with the *Invisible Man*-Faulkner relationships, it does offer the best larger perspective of Faulkner's view of the Negro in America. Finally, *Intruder in the Dust* might be used to see the "moderate" Southern view of slow melioration of the Negro's plight; allied to this, one might note the testy we-will-solve-our-own-problem attitude as illustrated by Gavin Stevens' overwhelmingly long-winded speech to Charles Mallison late in the novel. Also one could demonstrate the South's counter need not only to see the Negro as a cipher or an animal, but also to render him invisible—an essential Ellison thesis.

In *Shadow and Act* Ellison has acknowledged the seminal influence of Eliot's *The Waste Land* upon his development; the poem, he says "seized" his mind. It moved him deeply while its meanings eluded him, he explains, and he pursued his search for meaning by examining the notes and analyzing the structure of the poem itself. He consciously continued his literary pursuits by first moving to authors allied in time and attitude to Eliot and then to a gradually wider, but comprehensive, reading of American literary masterpieces. He became, through this careful reading, a knowledgeable literary critic and—partly through examination of craftsmanship of these authors—a practicing literary artist. Without exploring the Eliot-Ellison relationship minutely, it is still evident that the waste-land view of the twentieth century must have been congenial to the young Tuskegee student in White America. Further, Ellison's early interest and initial career aim was in the field of musical composition. He comments that the rhythms in *The Waste Land* "were often closer to those of jazz than were those of the Negro poets" (p. 162). These two strains then—the waste-land view of the world and the rhythms of the poem—might serve as the basis for valid comparisons. A reading, too, of Eliot's "Tradition and the Individual Talent" might offer insights into Ellison's use of the Negro's cultural and social traditions, areas which Ellison has explored more fully than any other contemporary writer of fiction.

Concerning the literature since World War II, Ellison's preoccupation with identity mirrors the work of several outstanding talents. As is the case with several serious modern novels, Ellison's *Invisible Man* substantiates John Alridge's thesis in his *After the Lost Generation* that "the quality and intensity of a literary work will depend, to a very large extent, upon the success with which the writer can find and communicate his private truth in the public truth of his age." [7] Robert Bone has pointed out that in his novel Ellison makes clear that his private truth is that because he is a Negro in America, he is deprived, even more than the white person, of his individuality; in the machine age, this is the microcosm for the larger truth that all of us are being deprived, at an increasingly accelerated pace, of our individuality (p. 197). Through this common theme one may note the similarity of *Invisible Man* to such novels as Updike's *Rabbit, Run*, Bellow's *The Adventures of Augie March* and *Herzog*, Malamud's *The Assistant*, Barth's *Gile's Goat-Boy* and Heller's *Catch-22*.

Examination of Ellison's work with that of such recent and major Negro novelists as Richard Wright and James Baldwin is, of course, another possibility in dealing with American novels and *Invisible Man;* their work, however, does not approach the artistic stature of Ellison's novel, and since Ellison considers himself an artist first and a Negro second, perhaps it is wiser to leave this avenue of examination unexplored here.

John Aldridge's statement concerning the loss of identity in Western society may be directly applied to *Invisible Man*, where invisibility is Ellison's symbol for loss of self. The novel becomes in Robert Bone's words "a stubborn affirmation of the worth and dignity of the individual in the face of forces which conspire to render him invisible . . . and . . . is dedicated in spirit to the suffering, mangled, helpless, plucked victim of Authority, whose only defense against power is his own humanity" (p. 197). This message which declares man's worth and dignity in opposition to the impersonal terror of authority has been a theme ranging through American literature and life virtually from our nation's beginning.

---

[7] New York, 1958, p. 85.

Whether delivered by Jefferson, Emerson, Clemens, Hemingway or Bellow, it is always worth the re-affirming. When delivered by an American Negro author, while in the background sound such slogans as "Burn, Baby, Burn," "Black Power," and "White Black-lash," the message commands the most profound urgency in being disseminated. Our country, which has been guilty of a radical racial injustice, must attend to this injustice with courage and intelligence; there is an abundance of each in *Invisible Man*, and one way of paying our attention today is by reading and teaching it.

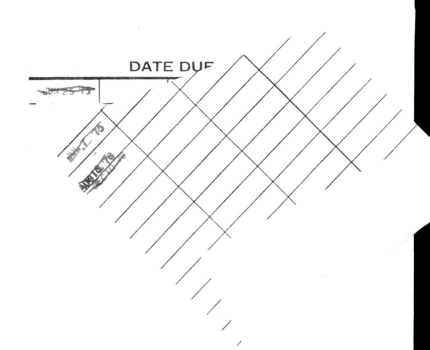

DATE DUE